The Charismatic Movement in the Church of England

D1614390

CIO PUBLISHING, Dean's Yard, London SW1P 3NZ

ISBN 0 7151 4751 X

Published 1981 for the General Synod of the Church of England
by CIO Publishing

Cover illustration by Barbara D'Arcy

Printed in England by Tasprint Ltd.

Foreword

In November 1978 the General Synod passed the following motion:

'That this Synod, noting the rise in recent years of the Charismatic Movement within the Church of England and being concerned to conserve the new life it has brought into many parishes, asks the Standing Committee to bring before the Synod a report which will explore the reasons for this upsurge, pinpoint the particular distinctive features of spirituality and ethos which the movement presents, and indicate both the points of tension which exist with traditional Anglicanism and also how the riches of the movement may be conserved for the good of the Church.'

(A fuller account of how Synod came to pass this motion and how the Standing Committee handled its task is to be found in Appendix 2.)

The members of the working group set up to draft this report by the Consultation at Ely convened by the Standing Committee were:

The Rev. Colin Buchanan
The Rev. Canon Colin Craston
The Rev. David Gregg
The Rev. Canon John Gunstone
Miss Christian Howard
Mr Derek Pattinson

Their first task was to identify the areas which needed to be covered and then to write not so much a final and definitive statement but rather a more popular summary of a spiritual movement still very much at work in our parishes. It soon became clear that, if this were to be a crisp and lively report, it would gain greatly by being substantially the work of one person. The other members of the group therefore prevailed upon the Rev. Colin Buchanan to undertake a draft of the report (though he, in turn, would wish the rest of the group to acknowledge the liberal editing of his contribution, which they are pleased to do). The group is grateful to him and to many others who have helped with their contributions and advice, particularly Canon Rex Davis, the Rev. Michael Harper, the Bishop of Pontefract, the Rev. John Richards and the Bishop of Wakefield, though the working group as a whole takes responsibility for the report's final form and content. It should be noted that some, but not all, members of the group are actively involved in the Charismatic Movement.

COLIN CRASTON
Chairman of the Working Group.

CONTENTS   *Page*

What is the Charismatic Movement?

Many, if not most, of the main denominations of the world church have over the last quarter of a century experienced a new spiritual movement, sometimes called the 'Charismatic Movement', sometimes the 'Charismatic Renewal', sometimes simply 'The Renewal'. Because it is a 'movement' it does not admit of clear boundaries or definitions. It is easier to recognise than to define, easier to describe by its phenomena than to isolate under a magnifying-glass, easier to experience than to report scientifically. If the word 'charismatic' is included in the title, then it appears to make *charismata*[1] too central to the movement; but if 'charismatic' is omitted, then the whole movement starts to lose its identity in discussion. Of these two horns of the dilemma, it is slightly more useful to be impaled on the former, and keep the word 'charismatic' in the title. There will still be difficulty in identifying what makes the charismatic movement the charismatic movement, but at least it will not be muddled with anything else.

Consider the following book titles (each one drawn from a biblical text): *You He made alive; Greater things than these; New Heavens, New Earth; As at the beginning; One in the Spirit; Remove the heart of stone; Not mad, most noble Festus; A people for his praise; When the Spirit comes; Locusts and wild honey.* Here, in a random series of titles mostly from within the movement, we begin to sense a flowing tide of Christian believers characterized by spiritual life, active and visible amongst them, by a strong sense of the power of God at work on earth (often in miraculous ways) amongst them, by an upward-looking faith, by a claim both of continuity with the early days of the apostolic church and also an openness to the future, and by a preoccupation with God himself, even at the risk of seeming to lose touch with the 'reality' of the more earthbound believers and unbelievers. If these titles reflect a movement, then the meeting of man and God — in particular the Spirit of God — is absolutely central to its concerns. The varied *charismata* may be an expression of that meeting in such a way that 'charismatic' becomes a loose shorthand way of identifying the movement. But it remains inexact as a descriptive title — the central feature of the movement is an overwhelming sense of the presence and power of a God not previously known in such a combination of otherness and immediacy. Nevertheless, we join the findings of the BCC's consultation on the value of charismatic renewal (held in December 1978):

'(In the early sessions) it had become apparent that there was no immediately acceptable definition for "charismatic renewal", either to those who felt themselves part of it or to those observing it.'[2]

It is our hope that sufficient description and evaluation, as those in the chapters following, will clearly identify the areas of the Church of England where there has been 'charismatic renewal' in the recent years. We recognize the difficulty of defining, but both refuse to be distracted by it, and also hope that as the report progresses we shall enable *recognition* to supplant *definition*.

There is an alternative technical term on offer. Sometimes the word 'Pentecostal' is employed, instead of 'charismatic'. This adjective, pointing as it does to the coming of the Spirit in power upon the infant church, has a more general connotation than 'charismatic'. However, its actual denominational and other usage has given it a fairly specific denotation, though modern 'charismatics' are often distinguished from more traditional Pentecostals by the prefix 'neo-', as 'Neo-pentecostals', which usually denotes charismatics in the mainstream Christian Churches, charismatics who have not become members of 'Pentecostal' churches. One of the problems with these terms is that, on most Christian analyses, they are apparently still capable of much wider application. 'We are all charismatics', said Donald Coggan, preaching to the conference for spiritual renewal at Canterbury just before the 1978 Lambeth Conference. This is so obviously true, yet so obviously unhelpful if it removes all descriptive labels. There has been — there is — such a movement. And we do need distinctive terminology such as the original General Synod motion gave us if we are to describe a distinctive movement at all.

However, this insistence that we are reporting a true movement with distinctive phenomena should not be read as a glib assertion that the task of reporting is easy. The Spirit of God works internally in the people of God — but the internal is difficult to report. The movement runs across denominational barriers (often weakening or lowering them in the process) — but we have to report on the Church of England as though it could be compartmentalized. A movement by definition moves on — but we have to stop the clock and report on a specified day, catching our subject as a still photo when a movie camera would have been more appropriate. Our soundings have been partial, our understanding limited, our time pressed, and our outlook (no doubt) over-subjective.

At the same time, the years from 1960 to 1980 have seen no less than 104 official or semi-official denominational reports (some national, some regional, some international) on 'the charismatic renewal', to judge solely from those published in the three volumes entitled *Presence, Power, Praise* edited by Kilian McDonnell.[3] This confirms our confidence that there *is* a distinctive movement, and that a report *is* a way of encapsulating it. We also note that Anglicanism barely figures in the list of 104 documents. So the Church of England is hardly precipitate in stopping to look at the spiritual upsurge which has been occurring within its corporate life in these two recent decades. And our investigations strongly confirm that it not only has been happening, but also, despite some recurrent schismatic tendencies, it has been happening to and among Christians who assert that this experience of the Spirit is the proper outcome of their Anglicanism, that the charismatic movement belongs within the Church of England and its

2

members are not to be driven out. They feel that the whole Church of England stands to gain by a determined holding on in love to what the movement has to offer, and to the hot-headed zealots it may throw up. We concur with this, and look for much growth in true spirituality to flow from this channel of God's power at the heart of our corporate Christian life.

CHAPTER 2

An Outline History

AN AUTHENTIC STRAND?

Without prejudice to the nature of Christianity in the first century — which is the very issue we are considering — it seems clear that, prior to the Reformation in Western Christianity,[1] the Church tended towards a very structured life, hierarchical in its ministry, formal (and even fossilized) in its liturgy, conservative in its temperament, and sacerdotal in its clericalism. One gets the impression that there was an authentic strand of New Testament Christianity which was being suppressed, although now and again it surfaced in outbursts of the Spirit, when visions and dreams and miracles and other 'non-rational' elements emerged. Montanism at the end of the second century represents the first major protest against the tendencies, but there were few similar movements in later years.[2] Such as there were — as, e.g., the Cathari or the Albigensians — are known to us largely or entirely from the reports of their persecutors, and may therefore not be accurately described.

The Reformation, whilst in general it produced mainstream Churches just as committed to order and decorum as the Roman Catholic Church, did open up sufficient room for other groups to emerge at intervals. Thus some of the Anabaptists of the sixteenth century on the Continent, or even of the Quakers (significant name!) in England in the seventeenth, were 'experience-centred' and showed it, in a way that reformed Anglicanism or Presbyterianism did not. Indeed, if we may take a case, the Church of England Prayer Books of the sixteenth and seventeenth centuries relied upon that famous 'charismatic' chapter I Corinthians 14 for just two points — to prove that unknown languages (sc. Latin!) should not be used in the congregation, and to prove (blessed be the Anglican Reformers) that all things should be 'done decently and in order' (I Cor. 14.40). On balance this seems an unbalanced presentation of the apostle's teaching.

There were unexpected phenomena — including groaning and crying aloud — amongst the early Methodists (though Wesley himself tended to attribute anything that interrupted his preaching to the devil rather than to the Spirit!), and there was distinct teaching amongst the Irvingites that such phenomena were right and godly.[3] But still in both the eighteenth and nineteenth centuries such questions were peripheral to general church life, and decorum and clericalism generally reigned.

There was, however, one phenomenon amongst evangelicals which may be of significance. In 1875 there was founded the Keswick Convention, which became a focus for the 'holiness' movements stemming from Wesley. Although no emphasis on *charismata* emerged, there *has* been a strong teaching of a two-stage idea (rebirth, and receiving the fulness of the Spirit) of entry into full Christian experience, and a whole sub-culture has been produced. This movement has also proved remarkably compatible with the East African Revival movement of the last forty years — a movement

4

which, whilst it has not been 'charismatic' in any overt way, has laid great weight upon the *experience* of 'walking in the light' and has often been recognized in the charismatic movement in England as a very near neighbour in Christ.

THE PENTECOSTALS BEGIN

The beginning of Pentecostalism as a world phenomenon is traceable to the beginning of the twentieth century. The Bethel Bible College in Topeka, Kansas was the scene of a build-up of prayer and enquiry towards an understanding of the baptism of the Holy Spirit. On 31st December 1900 the staff and students concluded that the baptism was evidenced by 'speaking in tongues'. They fell the further to prayer, and that evening — the last evening of the nineteenth century — they began to lay hands on each other, and to speak in tongues. Within a few years of this there came the beginnings in 1906 in Los Angeles (in a stable in Azusa Street) of what has now become the fellowship of denominations designated as Pentecostalism. The new feature of the teaching was the association of the experience of 'speaking in tongues' with the reception of the 'baptism in the Spirit' — itself a second stage in Christian initiation which might follow on years after the experience of conversion or first conscious belief.

Within a generation Pentecostalism had taken root as a forceful movement in many lands. In Britain revivals had prepared the ground, notably the Welsh revival of 1904 (associated with the name of Evan Roberts), which spread to Scotland by 1908. Frederick Dale Bruner writes, 'The Welsh revival appears to have been the last gap across which the latest sparks of the holiness enthusiasm leapt, igniting the Pentecostal movement'.[4]

History records one and only one Anglican parish which was involved in these early years. That parish was Monkwearmouth, Sunderland, in the diocese of Durham. The Vicar was one Alexander Boddy, who was influenced by both Evan Roberts and the Keswick Movement. A pentecostal revival broke out under his ministry in Autumn 1907, and seems to have continued for several years. It is marked to this day by an inscription on the wall of the Church Hall:

September 1907

WHEN

THE FIRE OF THE LORD

FELL

IT BURNED UP THE DEBT

With this one tiny (if notable) exception, there seems to have been a general rule that the formation of Pentecostal Churches both proved and caused a polarization. If individuals came into a 'pentecostal' experience, it was likely to be through the teaching and ministry of Pentecostals. If it happened in other ways or other contexts — and particularly in the mainstream Churches — then the individuals were likely either to be

5

counselled to forget it, or themselves to gravitate towards more sympathetic surroundings. Pentecostals remained a very distinct strand of church life, generally shunned in the first half of this century in England as not only erroneous, but also brazen, fanatical, anti-intellectual (which no self-respecting Anglican could ever be!), separatist, and 'holier than thou'. It must be remembered that these fifty years were ones where Anglicans found themselves with great difficulties in relating to the mainstream Free Churches — to relate to such a bizarre enterprise as Pentecostalism was rarely even on the mental agenda.

It would be difficult to chart here the various forms that the Pentecostal denominations have taken in England — forms varying according to internal doctrinal variations, and sometimes according to different forms of church policy. Some well-known names are 'The Assemblies of God', 'The Elim Foursquare Gospel Church', 'The Pentecostal Church', and so on. In recent years there have been added various West Indian titles, 'New Testament Church of God', etc.[5] And there are countless small independent assemblies which could broadly be called 'pentecostal' in their teaching and ethos. In many cases the charismatic elements have become highly stylized and very formal.

On a world-scene there have been areas, notably in South America, where Pentecostalism has been more obviously a church of the people — e.g., the main protestant alternative to Roman Catholicism — than in England. In such cases the leaders have found themselves with a sense of ecumenical responsibility which has not been discernible in England. Thus it was that in 1953, Bishop Lesslie Newbigin, a Christian statesman with a world-view, became the first mainstream churchman to treat Pentecostals seriously as part of the world-wide church. He did this in his Kerr lectures of November 1952, published as *The Household of God* by SCM press in 1953. Here he argued that there are *three* broad manifestations of Christianity to be found on the earth's surface — represented by adherents of the 'body' (or institution), viz. Roman Catholicism, by adherents of the word, viz. Protestantism, and adherents of the Spirit, viz. Pentecostalism.[6] This argument, which is central to the whole pattern of his lectures and by no means a mere passing thought, marked a milestone in the mainstream Churches' understanding of Pentecostalism, and the impression was reinforced when the first applications for membership of the World Council of Churches from Pentecostal Churches were received in the years following. (The first were received into membership at the third Assembly of the WCC at New Delhi in 1961.) It has to be acknowledged, however, that the progress of relationships between Pentecostals and mainstream Churches world-wide has still not progressed very far.

WITHIN ANGLICANISM

Michael Harper[7] traces the first influence of Pentecostals upon the mainstream Churches to the ministry of David du Plessis[8] in the 1950s. This

6

may have made for more openness towards Pentecostalism by such Churches. But the most significant beginnings within Anglicanism seem to have occurred more or less independently of such ministry, though within the suburbs of the city of Azusa Street — Los Angeles.[9] There, an outbreak of the characteristic phenomena of Pentecostalism occurred in 1959-60 in the parish of St Mark's, Van Nuys, under the ministry of Dennis Bennett (himself 'baptized in the Spirit' through the witness of a lay couple from a neighbouring Episcopal Church). And Dennis Bennett taught that the Pentecostal experience was no reason for leaving Episcopalianism, but rather for renewing one's witness within it. He also claimed that there were then 'dozens of Episcopal parishes' where a similar experience was known.[10] And it looks as though that was the beginning of the charismatic movement within the Episcopal Church. It is a movement which has gone from strength to strength, and grown its own associations and journals, held its own conferences, and linked hands with other charismatics throughout the world.

WITHIN THE CHURCH OF ENGLAND

The years immediately following these beginnings in the USA saw similar happenings in the Church of England— though with the distinction that what had in America come to high and sacramentalist churchmen came in England in the first instance to evangelical and Biblically-minded churchmen. An important influence in this was the testimony of that diehard protestant theologian, the Anglican Philip Hughes. He was editor of the evangelical quarterly *The Churchman,* and after a visit to California in 1962 spoke and wrote enthusiastically about what he had seen there amongst high churchmen. But it is unlikely that his contribution was decisive — rather it contributed to a movement that was already flowing. St Mark's, Gillingham, St Mark's, Cheltenham, and St Paul's, Beckenham all received publicity for outbreaks of 'tongues' in the years 1962-64, and the Anglican public at large became vaguely aware that something new and extraordinary — something not quite British and certainly not quite Anglican — had found a home within the Church of England. A particular focus of debate about the 'baptism in the Spirit' occurred on the staff of the 'Mecca' of evangelicalism, All Souls, Langham Place. Three of the curates in the years 1962-64 were John Lefroy, Michael Harper and Martin Peppiatt, who all became convinced of the pentecostal work of the Spirit through their experience and their understanding of Scripture. The Rector, John Stott, and some other members of staff (as, e.g. Julian Charley) were unconvinced, and were concerned that the teaching of the baptism in the Spirit was not thoroughly conformable to scripture, and would be highly divisive in practice. The staff held several thorough debates on the work of the Spirit in an endeavour to find a way through in unity, but the issue only died down following the departure of Martin Peppiatt overseas and the resignation of Michael Harper to found the Fountain Trust in 1964. This particular date and event marks a milestone in England.

7

It is clear with the benefit of hindsight that the early charismatics had inevitably to adopt a high profile. They could not but speak of the things they had heard and seen and experienced — and they had to speak in judgmental (if sorrowful) terms of the forms of Christianity which were, from this standpoint, arid and desert-like. Thus controversy was bound to be sharp, misunderstanding rife, and mutual appreciation hard to attain. The greater the enthusiasm of the newly renewed, the greater the wariness of the unrenewed. There seemed little prospect of a real joining of hands — and indeed few wanted it.

Thus the charismatic movement continued to grow, particularly among Anglican evangelicals, in the years 1964-1970. Names now well-known became associated with it — Michael Harper, John Collins, David Watson, David McInnes, Tom Walker, among others — tours were made in this country by Dennis Bennett and other Americans. Hodder started to publish books by these charismatic leaders, parishes overflowed with the distinctive marks of Pentecostalism, journals appeared, and the sense of a 'movement' in growing flood became strong. It would, however, have been perfectly possible to be a leading member of the Church of England and remain either unaware of the movement or sceptical as to its significance. Its scale was relatively small — even if interesting — in relation to the whole Church of England, and its distinctive features seemed bizarre, unwelcome, or even downright incredible, to those who only heard about them at second hand. The evangelical Anglican congress at Keele in 1967, whilst making statements on many other issues in the Church, gave no attention to the charismatic movement. The Anglican-Methodist Scheme, drafted in the years 1965 to 1968, was equally silent. Even the *Growing into Union* team[11] in 1970 treated the crucial issue of unity for the Church of England as an honest juncture between catholics and evangelicals without reference to any third strand of spirituality in the Church.

During the first five years of the 1970s various changes occurred in the nature of the movement as it flowed on and found new channels. A few of these may be tabulated in order to convey the feel of events.

1. An interest in the movement arose from the outside, an interest which both spread knowledge of the movement and also posed certain questions to it. One of these was J. D. G. Dunn, lecturer in New Testament at Nottingham University. His first book, *Baptism in the Holy Spirit,* arose from his doctoral thesis of 1968, and was published by SCM in 1970. In his preface he wrote that, despite the heavy criticism he felt bound to make of the Pentecostal doctrine of baptism in the Spirit, yet also

   'The Pentecostal contribution should cause Christians in the "main-line" denominations to look afresh with critical eyes at the place they give to the Holy Spirit in doctrine and experience . . . . .'.

   The index reveals little in the way of Pentecostal writers within the

8

Church of England whose writings were under review, save only Michael Harper. It is a work of serious scholarship, and there existed little Anglican charismatic scholarship worthy of his probing and correcting. Yet the general position held is clearly under review, and from one point of view Dunn's book is a landmark, presenting the charismatic movement for the first time as worthy of serious refutation, rather than negligent dismissal, at a central doctrinal point.

A similar dignification of the movement came from Walter Hollenweger. His big book, *The Pentecostals,* originally published in German in 1969, but translated, abridged, and brought up to date in 1972 for the English edition, also treated Pentecostalism (whether as a separate denomination or within the mainstream Churches) as a serious and stable feature of the Christian landscape, deserving of close study, and, in Hollenweger's work, certainly getting it. The book operates on a world scene — indeed it has but one page on events in the Church of England, out of a total of 572 (or of 287 in the 'history' section of the book). But it undoubtedly gave status to the movement, and the 'Belief and Practice' section carefully analysed the central teaching and distinctive behaviour of the Pentecostals. If the worldwide movement started to arrive on the landscape of the historic Churches with Newbigin, it finished arriving with Hollenweger.

2.   In the Church of England the movement spread out from its evangelical point of departure. Other traditions experienced the breath of renewal — sacramental traditions, and liturgical movement practitioners, both alike finding a new experience of God within their existing frameworks. It was noised about that even the Church of Rome now had charismatics — and it had.[12] None could be safely self-excluding simply on the grounds that this was contrary to his or her tradition. The traditions themselves were being revitalised.

At times apparently spontaneous outbreaks occurred. One notable example was that at St Hugh's, Lewsey, Luton. In 1971, under the ministry of Colin Urquhart, this became the scene of a Pentecostal outpouring simply through internal experience and mutual ministry. Colin Urquhart records in his autobiographical book, *When the Spirit Comes,*[13] that at the time neither he nor his congregation had any awareness of similar events elsewhere — further proof both that the growing movement of the 1960s was still relatively unknown in the Church of England and also that its growth did not all come from human influence and 'knock-on' effects.

An interesting parallel event was the 'renewal' of the Bishop of Pontefract, suffragan bishop of Wakefield. He tells his story in *Bishop's Move,*[14] and although he was greatly influenced by charismatic home meetings, his own catholic background and episcopal standing would not have made him a likely candidate for this change. He became a 'card-carrying' charismatic in 1973, and became also a staunch advocate of renewal *within* parish life, and renewal *within* the structures of the church ('with an occasional trip out for a "bless-up" if needed'!). In marked contrast with many overseas Provinces of the Anglican Communion, he remains, at the time of writing, the *only* Church of England bishop (diocesan or suffragan) known to admit his 'card-carrying' status, and thus represents an important rallying-point for confidence for Church of England charismatics.

3. The movement gained force from the popularizing of its distinctive music. The years from 1970 to 1975 saw the songs of the Christian roadshow *Come Together* overtaken by the overtly charismatic *Sound of Living Waters* (1974) and later *Fresh Sounds* (1976) — both edited by Jeanne Harper and Betty Carr Pulkingham, wives of men mentioned earlier.

4. The years from 1970 onwards saw a real attempt by charismatics and non-charismatics to find their way back into fellowship with each other from somewhat polarized positions. An outward symbol of this was the approach in 1974 by Michael Harper to John Stott which culminated in the encounter between the Fountain Trust and the Church of England Evangelical Council in 1975, and which led in turn to the publication of the report *Gospel and Spirit*.[15] A similar initiative from the British Council of Churches a year or two later, whilst in this case neither side was overtly Anglican, led to a somewhat different report.[16] But the crucial thing in each case was the desire to have the dialogue, both for clarification of misrepresented positions, and for mutual enrichment.

It is perhaps too early to put the years 1976-1980 under review, as we stand too close to events to evaluate them easily. But some of the following points should be noted:

1. The upturn of numbers offering for ordination in the Church of England in these years may well be due to an increased flow from charismatic circles.

2. The general 'loosening' of public worship which has come with modern language services and modern hymns has often led to a new freedom in Sunday worship amongst charismatics.

3. Interest in the movement, as the passing of the motion in General Synod which led to this report attests, has spread into all areas of the Church of England. It is evident that since the 1975 elections to Synod there have been quite a number of 'card-carrying' charismatics within the Synod itself.[17]

4. The sense that the movement is happening *among us* (and not 'over there') has enabled dioceses to include teaching on charismatic renewal in POT courses, Colleges to include teaching on charismatic spirituality in their ordination courses, and more and more Anglicans at every level in the Church to treat the movement as something normal rather than bizarre, thus hastening its full acceptance by the Church.[18]

5. Nevertheless, the trends set out above have had certain implications, some of which are not always so welcome:

(a) As the charismatic movement has become more domesticated in the Church of England and other mainstream churches, there has been a tendency for the more independently-minded practitioners to move into the 'House Church Movement' — forming what is beginning to look like a new charismatic 'denomination' (See Appendix 6)

(b) The second and third generation of believers in charismatic parishes may often welcome their spiritual inheritance without feeling the same necessity to exhibit 'tongues' and 'prophecy' on all possible occasions — and this in turn may deprive the newcomers of those security-giving signs or 'recognition-symbols' which have been part and parcel of the development of the movement.

(c) There has been a growing awareness of the pan-Anglican character of the movement, and this has been evidenced in the pre-Lambeth Conference for Spiritual Renewal at Canterbury in July 1978, the formation from that Conference of the trust 'Sharing of Ministries Abroad' (SOMA), and the further conference in Singapore in February 1981. Each of these has seen a heavy involvement from Anglicans in the USA, South Africa (where the Church of the Province of South Africa has been widely and deeply affected by the movement through the 1970s), Australia, and other places — often more (and certainly with more bishops) than from the Church of England.

(d) Paradoxically, or possibly consequentially, there has been a falling off of the the role of the Fountain Trust in England. The Trust, which, it will be remembered, is almost coeval with the movement in the Church of England, has technically been inter-denominational, but has in fact catered for a large Anglican constituency. The trustees began to sense in the latter years of the 1970s that their distinctive role was coming to an end, and in September 1980 they took the courageous decision to cease operations on 31st December 1980 (the last day of the decade!), in order to emphasize that renewal is as much the on-going task of the local church as the specialist task of an agency. The various institutional features of the Fountain Trust were handed on to other agencies to continue.[19]

(e) However, the question continues to arise whether the Church of England itself needs some specifically Anglican agency, even if it proves to be a low-profile and unambitious servicing enterprise. At the time of writing there is planned a conference of Anglican charismatics (and fellow-travellers) to take place at Swanwick in September 1981. One question this conference will have to consider is the desirability and constitution of any such agency.

We conclude this historical survey with some vignettes of the progress of the charismatic movement in various parishes and other institutions of the Church of England over the period under review.

Some Personal/Corporate Experiences

The Working Group asked a selection of parishes and institutions, through their present incumbents/wardens, to submit materials concerning:—

(a) The date and character of the rise of the movement within their parish/institution.

(b) A description of features of parish/community life most affected by this.

(c) Problems which have occurred.

(d) Evaluation of any benefits.

(e) Future goals.

(f) Anything else of interest.

We now reproduce four varying but fairly representative replies in full, and extracts from several others, related to the points mentioned:—

1. ST MARGARET, ASPLEY, NOTTINGHAM

(a) *Date and Character of the Rise of the Movement within the Parish*
There is no clear cut period that can be singled out but certain factors played their part:—

(i) The formation of regular healing services in 1970 through the ministry of the curate.

(ii) The personal renewal of the vicar, and soon after of his wife, in 1972.

(iii) In the summer of 1973 about 15-20 people were renewed in the Holy Spirit largely as a result of reading Dennis Bennett's *Nine O'clock in the Morning* and they joined the almost moribund Bible and prayer group which had started about 16 years before.

(iv) A small group had been meeting early in the mornings once a week to pray for the renewal and mission of the Church. This had started in 1970.

(b) *Features of Parish Life Most Affected*
Initially the old Bible and prayer group became the centre of renewal in the parish, and grew until it seemed right in 1975 to split into house groups. These groups have changed over the years but the personal renewal of the members is at the heart of their life. One such group held in the house of and led by a couple deeply committed to charismatic renewal grew to a membership of about 40 which included visitors from other churches.

The healing services became more 'faith-full' and as members grew became increasingly more celebratory in character with up to 250 attending. Increasingly these services were ministering to people from outside the

12

parish and it was recognized that part of the ministry of St Margaret's was to stimulate renewal in other churches over quite a wide area. Any tendency for the Church membership to become eclectic was strenuously resisted (over 85 per cent of the Church electoral roll lives in the parish). This 'extended' ministry began through the healing services but was continued through a series of large 'Celebrations' (up to 1,500 attending) held in 1977-1979.

In the last five years a series of six-week seminars, based on the Ann Arbor 'Life in the Spirit' seminars has taken place about three times a year. About 200 have attended these 'New Life' courses which have been the means of many coming to know Christ and being baptized in the Spirit.

The worship of the church was initially not greatly touched — though many said that the vicar's preaching had a new authority! However, from 1976 onwards some of the insights into worship from the Weekday Fellowship meetings and healing services began to become evident. Although the structure of the service remained (Series 3 Parish Communion and 1662 Evensong) they became freer, more experimental and participatory, though it was seldom that the gifts of the Spirit were exercised.

Over the last eight years numbers at Parish Communion have risen from around 60 to an average of 140. There has been a noticeable drop in the average age of the congregation.

Evangelism has featured much more strongly both within and outside the parish. For instance between 1975-1978 more than 20 teams involving 70-80 different people were sent out to other churches, mainly for weekend missions.

(c) *Problems which have Occurred*

(i) There have been tensions between those who wished things to remain as they were and those who relished the more informal atmosphere. The vicar bore the brunt of these tensions and did not let them erupt in the congregation so that the change that has taken place has been remarkably smooth. However there are some, mainly the older long standing members, who feel a bit let down as the old familiar landmarks have largely disappeared. But most of the older members of the congregation, while not necessarily participating in the renewal, have shown much graciousness and rejoice in the younger people in the congregation, and the gradual introduction of new ideas. There has been an overall insistence on love as the bond of Christian fellowship.

(ii) A 'Charismatic' church with a well-known ministry of healing tends to attract the neurotic, inadequate and difficult folk. At times they have swamped the pastoral resources of the Church and too much time and attention has been devoted to them to the detriment of the leadership of the Church as a whole, and the pastoral care of other people within the parish. However these are people whom it is right for the Church to minister to.

(iii) It has not always been easy to gauge the right balance between an emphasis on decentralisation in house groups and the coming together of the Body of Christ in a central midweek fellowship. Sometimes the emphasis has been in one direction, sometimes the other. We have found a need to have a major reassessment about every other summer.

(iv) A fair number within the Church (including some who hold office) have stood aside from renewal, finding their own lives little affected by it.

(d) *Evaluation of Benefits*

(i) From the beginning renewal has had a strong social content. A striking example of this is given in (f) below.

(ii) Many people have found Christ as a living reality in their lives. Numbers of people (running into 100s) have become Christians from inside and outside the parish. Others through the renewal have found their Christian lives transformed, their worship enlivened and their service empowered.

(iii) The age structure of the congregation (in 1970 there were only a handful between 18 and 50) more closely reflects the structure of the parish.

(iv) The predominance of people from private housing is less with a growing number from the council estates part of the fellowship.

(v) Through the ministry of healing many benefits, physical, emotional, spiritual, have been brought to numerous people. Because of the ministry of St Margaret's other churches (mainly, but not exclusively Anglican) have started a similar ministry.

(vi) Through the minstry of St Margaret's God has been 'put on the map' as far as many people are concerned. They may not like to be reminded of His presence but they can no longer ignore Him.

(e) *Future Goals*

(i) To develop a leadership structure where the vicar is 'Primus inter pares' and which is capable of sustaining further growth. This demands a tighter framework within which pastoral care is exercised and a greater understanding of the nature of authority and discipline within the security of the love of Christ.

(ii) Equipping all the saints for the work of ministry, thus emphasizing the importance of teaching and discerning the gifts and ministries that are being given to individuals and groups. In particular the recent burden for evangelism needs to be sustained and extended and a strategy for evangelism, particularly applicable to the Council estates, needs to be worked out.

(iii) A new perspective in giving needs to be grasped.

(iv) Exploring the whole area of 'Lifestyle' both as to the relevance of 'community' within a parish and the implications of the needs of the Third World etc. in an ordinary suburban mixed parish.

(f) *Anything Else of Interest*
Between 1974-1977 there were certain tentative experiments regarding the development of families living in 'Community'. One such group of three families has formed a Trust which now runs a shop in the main shopping area of the parish known as 'Green Pastures'. It is a means whereby nearly new clothes, furniture etc. is made available at very reasonable cost mainly for the benefit of families on the Council estates. It is run by a body of 40-50 volunteers drawn from Christians of all denominations. It is proving to be a wonderful contact point as well as expression of genuine co-operation among Christians of different traditions. It is one of the best means of breaking down barriers that we know of in Aspley.

Conclusion
None of this would have been possible without the inspiration of the Lord of the Church. The glory is His and not man's. Praise to His Name!

2. ST JOHN THE BAPTIST, HARBORNE, BIRMINGHAM
A dozen or so members of St John's met for prayer together with others from Birmingham Cathedral and a few other churches for a weekly time of prayer from 1967-70. In July 1970 these formed the nucleus of a prayer group at St John's Harborne which became known as 'Open to God'. The purpose of this prayer time was to wait upon God for his direction for the work of the parish and to receive for upbuilding and equipment in ministry any gifts that God might pour out upon us. Those at the meeting sought the grace of God, but it could hardly have been labelled 'charismatic' in its expression. The neutral title of the meeting indicated our desire for reality with God in our particular situation. There was no intention to be any sort of 'charismatic' bandwagon. The meeting was purposely held on church premises and not in an individual's home, so that it was open to all in the church, and we chose the discomfort of any early hour to ensure that those present had serious intent.
    Aspects of church life most affected by this gathering were:—

(a) *Evangelism.* We waited for direction about the pattern of evangelism for some six or seven months. We seemed called to set up home groups in order to encourage a sharing faith more openly among ourselves before going to outsiders. From these praying groups a witness team was called out about seven months later. Some forty or so formed the first team and the groups took on the character of missionary prayer groups, praying for the missionaries sent out into our own parish. After a year of experiment the evangelism took place in two bursts from October-December and from February-April each year. The parish was divided into six sections in order to enable proper follow-up and befriending of those who professed faith. Evangelistic preaching is geared to this annual campaign, and many in the church assist in administration, pre-visiting with a Vicar's letter, babysitting, prayer, etc. so that evangelism uses many varied gifts within the church. It is entirely lay-led, though the team is trained by the clergy each year. The whole parish is visited three times each year in addition to this intensive evangelism. Many have been won to Christ over the years, and the whole pattern stemmed from the prayer for renewal.

(b) *Worship.* This has been transformed in quality in answer to prayer and through the release of gifts of music, art and dance. There is participation in prayer and praise involving scores in the congregation. The mid-week prayer time grew from about 20 to 300 at its peak. If smaller home groups are included there are nearly 500 attending regular prayer groups, in all age ranges from young people to the extremely elderly. The main services are sometimes opened up to include congregational participation.

(c) *Ministry.* Many in the congregation have a ministry of counselling and care, and leaders of home groups are trained in the task of pastoring their groups. Each pair of leaders has a subsidiary pair of leaders in training, and ready to take over leadership of another group. As well as many experienced in evangelism through the witness team, we also have a trained pastoral care team who visit and care for the elderly and shut-in. We also have a number of leaders who are experienced in dealing with occult problems which frequently come to us from other parts of the diocese as well as from our own parish. Part of our social care is expressed in a Play Group run by one of the staff. In the development of this wider ministry the number of staff grew from two to six full-time and one half-time — all paid from our own funds. The giving has risen from an average of about £50 a week to an average of about £1,500 a week last year.

(d) *Plant.* The church has been enlarged to seat an extra 200 people, a youth centre has been built and additional housing for staff purchased — all since 1974.

(e) *Outreach.* Teams have travelled all over the country to other churches and the choir has toured Sweden and Denmark and will be singing in Finland this year. Clergy lead missions in various European countries, and over the last five years over 150 of the congregation have entered full-time missionary work abroad or have entered the ministry of the church at home.

The problems have been mainly in the area of eldership. This was approached very carefully with prayer and study over a whole year, but rivalries developed and very painful tensions arose, culminating in illness and breakdown. There was a considerable amount of misunderstanding. Two staff members left for other work and one lay elder moved away, and a new team was established. Good fellowship was restored and no-one is in any sort of continuing dispute. Apologies have been made all round, and eldership still functions.

Instead of eldership benefiting the church, there was a stage where it was taking many hours a week to keep relationships happy. Seen as part of the spiritual battle a time of trial might have been expected. We are now older and wiser, and limitations of health following the difficulties have led to even wider sharing of responsibilities so that now more people are ministering in the church than before.

The benefits renewal has brought are to be seen in the openness that Christians have with each other. There is a readiness to seek prayer counsel and ministry, and a much greater sense of interdependence than there was before. Many people are healed through spiritual ministry and many give themselves to this caring and healing task. Generous giving means that we are not hindered in ministry through lack of finance.

As far as future goals are concerned, our hope would be to share more realistically in some neighbouring inner ring area of the city. Many of our members teach and give health care in immigrant areas of the city, but we are growing towards a sense of responsibility towards our needy city beyond the bounds of our own parish. Our own area has few immigrants but many social problems — we are not a select suburb exactly — and we are concerned to take our full part in helping with Birmingham's problem areas. We are also concerned for the third world and have a number of our members serving in sensitive areas of South America and Africa.

Our aims are to be obedient, if we can, in doing the next thing God shows us to do. We feel that our call is to faithfulness in the small everyday matters, and we do not feel called to grandiose schemes and projects. We see many areas of need which we have not tackled in our parish, but we do not undertake anything which we cannot reasonably sustain. We have an emphasis on Christian families having time to keep together, and we are anxious not to make wrong demands of time on busy people. This means that we learn to live with the tension of leaving some good things undone through lack of workers, but it also means that those things we attempt to do, we seek to do as well as we can in the power of the Spirit and for Christ's glory.

3. ST HUGH, LEWSEY, LUTON

(a) The Renewal started at St Hugh's soon after a new Vicar came in 1970. He himself was experiencing a new opening out of his faith at the time and shared this with the church. A number of people were fairly quickly influenced and as they opened up their lives through confession and absolution and prayer for the gift of the Holy Spirit, began to know a much closer relationship with the Lord and to experience his activity in their lives. Gifts of the Spirit were manifested; tongues, prophecy, healing, etc. The movement spread, more and more people were affected and there was a growing sense of blessing and expectancy and a measure of excitement in the life of the church.

(b) An immediate effect was upon the prayer life of the church, people praying with more eagerness and reality, people praying with each other and in groups. Prayer groups sprang up. Worship was enlivened and began to be freed from too much formalism. Parish Communion remained much the same in structure (Series 3) and ceremonial (vestments

17

etc.), but a new spirit was recognisable in worship. Evensong gave way to Evening Praise, a freer service with guitar group, songs, free prayer and a concentration upon 'the Word'. The Vicar's preaching was powerful. People began to find a new love for the Bible and to want to know what God was saying in and through it. A greater sense of fellowship in the Body of Christ was engendered, people sharing their lives much more closely and intimately than hitherto. In due course this developed into a form of Community life, about 50 of the congregation sharing a common purse, pooling income and sharing houses where possible. People from outside the parish began to come to the church, some moved house into the area. Many visitors came, having heard of the new things happening, a number being converted and some healed. Before long a team led by the Vicar began to visit other churches to share a message of renewal and the Vicar himself came to be in great demand as a preacher and Conference speaker.

(c) Many problems have been encountered. In the early days there were those who could not accept the changes taking place, nor the message preached. Some left the church to go elsewhere, others stayed but rather on the edge of things. These were not cared for adequately. If you were not in on what was going on, you were out. The development of the community life caused further divisions. Relationships suffered from the fact that there were some in the community and some not. Some deep wounds and hurts were experienced and feelings of condemnation if you did not conform. There were some problems of over-intense spirituality, a losing sight of the Incarnational aspects of Christianity. Family life suffered in some quarters for a time, some giving more time to church life than was appropriate.

(d) In retrospect, it is apparent to the writer (who became Vicar in 1976) that the benefits of the renewal have outweighed the problems. Suggestions that such renewal would be a 'flash in the pan' and that personal conversion and healing would be short-lived have proved untrue. Ten years later, the great majority of those initially involved are still faithful and have grown remarkably more mature over the years and through the problems. Many have become valuable leaders, some have taken up full-time Christian work, six men offered themselves for ordination, four being accepted, two already ordained and two in training. People have come to see the need for renewal to be expressed in practical ways in work and family life. Many relationships have been healed and a great measure of unity restored in the church. There is also a more mature attitude towards the gifts of the Spirit, people having learned by trial and error and not a little suffering to 'test the spirits' and be wiser and more discerning. There is still much prayer for healing and much answered prayer too, but here again, we have come to see healing more in the light of God's ultimate purposes for man and not so much as a thing on its own.

(e) In the early days of the renewal there was a losing sight of the impor-

18

tance of the church as a parish church within the Anglican set up serving the locality. St Hugh's became rather a centre of renewal. It now becomes more a parish church again attracting many more people from the locality and not a few from the densely populated housing estate nearby. The aim is to be an alive local church with both a social and evangelistic concern for the people. The group life of the church has recently been restructured with these goals in mind, the parish being divided into areas and 'area fellowships' for the purpose of prayer. A 'Family Service' was started monthly which draws a large number of people from the locality and plays a part in what is a fairly welcoming baptism policy. There is a sense of expectancy that the church may have to care for an influx of new Christians in the near future. This is partly due to preparations for a mission in Luton later this year.

(f) One of the lessons learned here is that pastoral considerations can easily be overlooked in a renewal situation, that such renewal needs to be nurtured under a mature pastoral oversight and preferably in a shared leadership situation. We have sought to develop this here in recent years with great benefit to the ongoing life of the church. There has seemed to be no need to establish elders and so on, but we have worked within the normal Church of England structures so far as leadership and authority are concerned. The PCC is the final decision making body and the Standing Committee consisting of three clergy, Church wardens, Secretary, Treasurer and two elected representatives from the PCC meet at least twice a month for prayer and discussion concerning the general direction of church life. The area fellowship leaders also meet together frequently. Frequent meeting and consultation in which folk are free to express just what they think and feel seems to be essential to offset and deal with the many lively problems that a renewal situation presents. Otherwise pressure from strong individuals and groups can quickly upset the harmony and people begin to pursue independent ministries, at times unwisely. A shared leadership can test 'hot lines' to God, prophetic revelation etc. and discourage the spiritual manipulation that is sometimes a problem. The intense spirituality that is an occasional feature in charismatic renewal leads also to theological imbalances such as gnosticism and monophysitism. These need to be offset by repeated emphasis of the incarnational aspects of Christianity and the essential humanity of Jesus.

I have preferred to speak of renewal in Christian faith and life rather than of the Charismatic Movement, the latter term not being used much nowadays owing to its limitations as a description of what God is doing. However the phrase does indicate a release of gifts and there is no doubt that those so renewed do have much to give to the church. When they are encouraged and guided the church is richer for them. It is a personal reflection that the Spirit will need the institution and the institution will need the Spirit if the opportunities of this decade are to be grasped.

4. ST JOHN'S COLLEGE, NOTTINGHAM (from a member of staff)

I joined the staff of St John's College in 1970 at a time when the effect of the renewal movement in parishes was beginning to be reflected among ordinands. We had a number of students from flourishing charismatic evangelical parishes in areas such as Gillingham, York, and Chorleywood, although the general style of college was that of post-Keele evangelicalism. But some of these students — though not all! — were among the more impressive of the student body, in their spirituality, ministerial potential, and character; nor did they lack theological articulateness. This fact, along with the growth of the renewal movement in the church at large, pressed on the college as a whole the question of its attitude to the issues the movement raised for the church.

The issues, I think, were three. First, were the 'charisms' referred to in the NT to be expected to feature in the church today? Evangelical exegetical tradition said that they belonged uniquely to the NT period, but putative events now belied this and at least some of the college staff, while not having charisms such as tongues or prophecy themselves, accepted the prima facie evidence that God might be speaking through these charisms today. Opportunity was sometimes given for the exercise of tongues and prophecy in college chapel, and these charisms were occasionally used. I do not think that the college's theology of charisms has changed significantly over the decade; though on one side some staff and students emphasize that we should be actively seeking these charisms more, while others remain a bit sceptical (usually discreetly so) about the whole business.

Second, was Christian initiation essentially a one-stage or a two-stage affair? At the beginning of the decade the classic Pentecostal two-stage theory was prominent in renewal circles. On exegetical grounds, the college staff generally opposed that, and for a while this was simply a topic of disagreement which made the staff suspect in the eyes of people who had had their 'baptism in the Spirit'. We were just not quite 'there' spiritually. But in due course the renewal movement perhaps moved, and was open to different ways of describing the experience under discussion, and the college perhaps moved, being more willing to grant the importance of the experience of this kind which God gave to some people.

This leads to the third issue. Michael Harper visited college on one occasion in about 1973 and the staff invited him to coffee — nervously but fearful of seeming to ignore him. Someone asked what at heart he saw the renewal movement as about, and he replied 'It's about an experience of God'. Here it became clear that he was reasserting a traditional evangelical emphasis which could get lost behind the equally traditional but more rationalist interest in doctrine and the newer interest in ecclesiastical politics; and especially in the context of some questioning of traditional ideas about personal prayer in college in a late interacting with the secularist theology of the 1960s. Further, because it was a traditional evangelical emphasis, some who had experienced 'revivals' elsewhere (e.g. in East

20

Africa) could fairly easily find themselves at home in this new renewal movement.

There were some odd or worrying goings on. One or two of the charismatic students were inclined to find demons under every bed, and indulged in exorcistic activity in the neighbourhood. We gave lecture space to an itinerant healer who some students felt was manipulating students into an experience of being 'slain in the Spirit' (literally manipulating — he pushed them over!). On the other hand, the staff's uneases were generally received with glazed looks by charismatic students — what else was to be expected from people who hadn't had these experiences themselves? Consequently charismatic students still tended to hold 'private' meetings for the discussion and the exercise of gifts. Nevertheless we were apparently more open on these issues than most colleges, and it seems that word went round the charismatic parishes that this was the case, so that an increasing number of their ordinands chose to come here.

This ambivalent situation changed somewhat in the mid-seventies, when the renewal 'experiences' and the exercise of charisms became not merely tolerated by the staff but shared by at least some of them. One member of staff had his 'experience' as a result of hands being laid on him at dead of night at a theological colleges staffs' conference. But the change in the staff relationship to the movement came about also through the way staff appointments happened to work out during this period. There were also further changes in the renewal movement itself, so that it welcomed members of our staff who themselves still lacked the renewal 'experience' and the key charisms to speak at conferences and to write for its publications. This again increased the sense in college that we were for the renewal movement and not merely tolerant of it. Conversely, charismatic leaders participated in the planning of NEAC in Nottingham in 1977 and wrote Grove Booklets. And as the renewal ball rolled faster in the church and the number of ordinands influenced by it increased, so the proportion of them who came to St John's increased, so that they were probably a majority by the mid-seventies, and still are.

The college's affirmation of the movement meant that inside it the exercise of charisms became in principle a feature of mainstream college life rather than a practice indulged by a small minority in secret corners. Most weeks there would probably be some opportunity for the exercise of charisms in college chapel, and on a fair number of occasions (though perhaps never as many as evangelicals and charismatics outside thought) people brought tongues, followed by interpretation, prophecies, or 'pictures'. Once or twice there was 'singing in the Spirit'. The staff committed themselves to seeking to function as 'elders' who guided/oversaw this exercise of charisms and considered its contents afterwards.

A ministry of healing also developed during this period. Since March 1977 one Holy Communion service each term has included ministry of healing, sometimes with annointing. But the renewal movement had a

21

perhaps greater influence on the way people went about more private ministry. Even before the college moved to Nottingham in 1970, the approach to counselling developed by Dr Frank Lake had been of considerable influence in the college, and Dr Lake had aligned himself with many of the renewal movement's emphases. Various other comparable approaches to 'inner healing' developed during the seventies and came to be used in counselling in college. Renewal insights thus contributed to an ease and frutifulness in one-to-one ministry among staff, students, and their families, and to significant developments in our understanding of what life together as Christians means (even if we puzzle over what being 'a Christian community' can mean for a theological and training institution).

The college had long been interested in developing the use of art, music and drama in workshop and evangelism and this period also saw huge development in the musical side of college worship, especially through the work of two particularly able pianists/composers, and through the involvement in worship of a variety of able flautists, violinists, cellists, trumpeters etc. Often the music was now what lifted a service and gave people the feeling that they had met God there.

This period also brought the breaking down of some ecclesiastical barriers. The college received a flow of ordinands from the traditionally catholic Church of the Province of South Africa. Here the renewal experience and the enthusiasm for the scriptures which often issued from it seemed to make churchmanship issues insignificant. Conversely, the renewal influence gave added stimulus to an interest in colour, art, drama, and dance in worship. Towards the end of this mid-seventies period Robin Nixon, then Principal of St John's, chaired a joint working party of 'traditional' and charismatic evangelicals, which in 1977 agreed the report *Gospel and Spirit,* and it seemed more and more difficult to define the difference between charismatic and non-charismatic. Then in 1978 St John's appointed the Director of the Fountain Trust as Doctrine Lecturer and Vice-Principal, and this might have seemed to set the seal on the college's commitment to the renewal movement. In fact, however, this was a period in which the questions raised by the movement came to voice themselves more loudly than those it answered. We had received a number of prophecies etc. in college chapel, but never with the degree of freedom that people who were in the heart of the renewal movement longed for. Further, these messages mostly seemed to reflect only too clearly the background and inner personal needs of the messengers, and the number that (in my view) spoke with clear authenticity and challenge was very small. (Although I *do* recall a 'picture', given by one of my colleagues, of a duplicator churning out reams and reams of timetables, papers, and handouts, alongside a table spread for a banquet which nobody was coming to eat; and that spoke powerfully of how our life could be!)

We had heard many people testifying to the depth (and the finality) of what the Lord had done in their lives, but it was not generally manifest that this work was either particularly deep or final, and we heard increasingly students revealing the actual thinness of their current experience of God by their pleas to be given a place or a time or a method for prayer.

We saw some answers to prayer for physical healing, but also some similar prayers not answered (as when a student wife died of cancer) and some deep lessons learned and true 'healing' experienced through suffering, rather than through the removal of suffering. We noted however that the stress on experience of God and on God's love could easily lead to an inadequate awareness of the need to accept responsibility for one's behaviour and for commitment to changing it.

The end of the decade thus finds the college uncertain of the fruits of the renewal movement. Some staff and many students believe that we ought to be seeking more earnestly the realities which the renewal movement stands for. Others believe that we are called to get in perspective the real but partial insights of a movement which is now essentially over, and to look to the next thing God may be doing.

5. EXTRACTS FROM OTHERS

(a) *The rise of the Movement*

'In 1973 the Vicar began to share the pastoral care of the Parish with eight Lay Pastors . . . . In 1974, after six months intensive preparation, a Mission to the Parish was launched on Ash Wednesday . . . . On the Feast of Pentecost 1974 we prayed in faith and in hope that God would pour His Holy Spirit upon us as He had done on the Church in Jerusalem those many years ago. There was great peace over the whole gathering. Within weeks we had begun to experience the Baptism of the Holy Spirit, first among our staff and then spreading out through the whole congregation. There was a surging tide of excitement and expectancy.'

(Holy Trinity, Hounslow)

'In 1974 a Parish week-end conference was organised, the emphasis being upon the work of the Holy Spirit, what was meant by the Baptism with the Holy Spirit, and what were the gifts of the Spirit. During the course of this week-end many people experienced a new dimension of the work of the Holy Spirit within their own lives, being themselves filled with the Spirit and beginning to manifest the gifts. From this time on more people, of all age groups, were touched by the Holy Spirit, bringing a sense of renewal to each one. In light of this, it may be said that this particular week-end conference was a time when the rise of the Charismatic movement became more evident.'

(Canford Magna, Dorset)

'We met for six months of discussion and prayer before anything happened: then my wife was baptized in the Spirit, He was released with new power in my own experience and more and more people came into the same experience. This was in the Spring of 1972 and a weekend away for the parish — a kind of Retreat, but more discursive than silent, especially on this 'new' subject — enabled us to make much progress in renewal . . . . In June 1973 Graham Pulkingham brought 7 Fisherfolk for a week's 'Mission' and this really clinched our impact on church life and our church building was filled on several occasions.'

(St Margaret, Durham)

'The challenge of one layman who saw the initial "Call to the North" letter from the Archbishop of York (Donald Coggan), the then Archbishop of Liverpool (George Beck) and the Moderator of the Free Church Federal Council (John Huxtable) was straight from the shoulder — "Are we just to have that letter read out from the pulpit or are we going to do something about it?" . . . . We immediately started a Prayer Group — and I was joined by colleagues on the staff who felt the need, even though none of us would call ourselves, in Colin Buchanan's words, "card-carrying charismatics"!'

(St James' and Emmanuel, Didsbury, Manchester)

'I began my ministry in this parish at the beginning of 1970. My purpose from the outset until now has been that we should incorporate as far as possible insights of the charismatic movement without necessarily aligning ourselves self-consciously with the charismatic movement (or indeed any other movement). This purpose springs from a belief that it is most helpful to the people within the church and also those around us whom we seek to reach that we should aim at being Christians and being known as Christians rather than as belonging to a particular party. This intentional element of reserve may be responsible for the fact that certain elements of charismatic life have not gone as far as they might have done if we had been wholeheartedly part of this movement to the exclusion of other streams of life within the total church. Having said that, our life here has been very deeply affected by the insights of this movement.'

(St Stephen, East Twickenham)

(b) *Features most affected*
'By March 1978 the majority of our congregation were tithing their gross salaries and we were able to take steps to become self-supporting while greatly increasing our support for the Church overseas.'

(Holy Trinity, Hounslow)

'From that moment, new people started to come to church who had never been used to going to church before. They were buying bibles and were reading them. Many of the people who came were broken and hurt; people who needed so much love, and who are now themselves giving out that same love. It seemed as though everyone wanted to pray, to grow closer to God. I myself, for weeks after the experience I have related, spent all of my working day in church: in prayer, as the church grew . . . . On that blessed day I have told you about, and for some time afterwards, when the most beautiful things were happening, we had never heard of the Charismatic movement, and were amazed to find that this sort of thing is now happening throughout the world and in every denomination, from the Pentecostalists to the Roman Catholics.'

(Holy Trinity, Littleborough, Lancs.)

'. . . . as a Conference Centre we have all shades of the spectrum, and have come increasingly to appreciate them all as reflecting different aspects of our Father's love. Our personal sympathies make us warmly open to charismatics, but in no way exclusively biased as a 'charismatic' centre.'

(Blaithwaite House, Cumbria.)

'The features of the parish life most affected are a sense of corporateness; quality of relationships; and emphasis on every-member ministry resulting in a shared leadership (elders), a pattern of house-groups etc. In addition, there has been a considerable impact on the worship with many new songs being written, the use of various instruments, and a general sense of freedom in the presence of God. Prayer and worship are marked by the expectation that God is there and longs to bless and move in response to his people's prayers. Evangelism is now seen as a ministry of the whole body of Christ, many of those who are converted mentioning the Service or the sense of love, rather than the sermon, despite the fact that we have a gifted evangelist in David Watson. The area of the arts has blossomed; the creation of a full-time theatre company, professional quality musical plays being put on twice in recent years — written by members of the church; etc. At different times some members of the congregation have lived in extended households, and the issue of a simpler lifestyle has been a major feature in our thinking in recent years.'

(St Michael-le-Belfrey, York)

'It is, I believe, a result of this particular work of the Spirit that we have seen the need to promote love between our members as a primary task, and to rise above a contentment with teaching doctrines which do not produce love. You do not have to be within the charismatic stream to know and experience the love of God shed abroad in one's heart: however, I think that in our case this emphasis arose from this movement . . . . In weekday meetings for prayer and fellowship, there has been slowly developing a learning to wait upon God. I do not think that we would have achieved this dimension of prayer apart from the insights of this movement. It has helped to develop within us a desire to listen to God. This readiness to listen is doubtless obtained by many others without reference to this movement, but it seems that we needed some experience of the word of God being brought to us through gifts of the Spirit to obtain this listening attitude.'

(St Stephen, East Twickenham)

(c) *Problems encountered*
'A loving caring church attracts those seeking attention, and in true hysterical fashion are damaging when they cannot hold the centre of the stage'.

(Holy Trinity, Hounslow)

'The experience of Renewal brings expectation beyond the maturity of a congregation to fulfil. Answered prayer and abundant blessing can mislead people into a false expectation that there are going to be no problems between people and no weaknesses that will not be healed and that there will be endless growth, abundant success and ease.'

(Holy Trinity, Hounslow)

'Problems one would see arise from the Christian's innate tendency, once having received the grace of God, to want to continue running the new thing himself, rather than letting the Lord actually *be* Lord, and do the driving. The result is a Holy Spiritless imitation, which rings hollow, doesn't convince anyone else, and takes all the efforts of the group to keep it going. Results may include shallow "praise", ephemeral frothiness, or, more dangerously, extravagant claims as to what the Lord is reputed to be saying or doing. All this is no discredit to the charismatic movement as such, but yet another confirmation of the Scripture's view of the nature of man, and his behaviour in relation to grace. If the disasters hadn't worked out the way they have, it would be far more worrying!'

(Blaithwaite House, Cumbria)

'We have at different times had serious problems over the role of the gift of prophecy, the nature of pastoral authority or 'shepherding'; the practical difficulties of releasing individuals into the ministry of spiritual gifts and encouraging genuinely every-member ministry, rather than just the theory of it; something of a lack of social concern in the congregation, with a redemption-based theology lacking a creation-based perspective; some issues of lifestyle and simplicity have met with resistance in the congregation; and it has taken us a long time to work through the issue of women in authority, and we are by no means unanimous in this matter at present. One practical problem is that with an eclectic congregation which tends to attract those who are in professions which move them on every few years, we have a considerable turnover of a proportion of our congregation. Consequently, we can never assume that the faith and experience of the fellowship is based on all the lessons of the last 15 years — we constantly have to relay the foundation for some of our members.'

(St Michael-le-Belfrey, York.)

'I am often asked what problems have been caused by the Spirit's work among us. The answer is, of course, none. God the Holy Spirit has caused us no problems, nor has this movement. However, we have caused the Holy Spirit plenty of problems by our slowness to respond and to obey Him. All in all, I think it is fair to say that God in His mercy has preserved us with wonderful unity and harmony over these ten years. This to me is a miracle. Perhaps we would have had greater difficulties, if we had been bolder and more faithful to some of the directions in which God has been calling us. Areas of difficulty which I can recall are these. (i) Guidance. We have run into some tangles on our PCC over the question of guidance. I think we would have had a smoother course if we had not been involved in the insights of this movement. Our PCC found it difficult for a time to reach unanimity on the appointment of a full-time Youth Leader. The nub of the difficulty boiled down to differing concepts of guidance. The awareness that God speaks to us led to an expectation that all members must hear Him speaking to them. We have now learned that God often speaks to a small group over a particular issue, and the larger group learns to recognize the voice of God in the convictions of the smaller group. (ii) Worship. The vision which we have for freer more wholehearted and joyful worship leaves us with a sense of considerable dissatisfaction with the level of worship which we have at present. We would probably be much more content with where we are if we had not experienced some heights of worship through the Spirit's help. (iii) Dance group. We have had occasional short items of dance in our worship. This is not necessarily a charismatic thing, and the items were prepared rather than spontaneous. I know that a few members of our church found this difficult to swallow, although it brought joy and spiritual uplift to the great majority.'

(St Stephen, East Twickenham)

(d) *Benefits perceived*
'In the context of the house groups, as the people get to know each other, they are sharing at deeper levels, thus enabling a greater ministry of caring and sharing to be experienced. The needs of people are being met both at a spiritual and practical level, not only by the staff but by lay involvement at every level.'

(Canford Magna, Dorset)

'Benefits . . . . dozens of them! Previously defeated individuals brought into victory and stability; folk with 'nerves' on a diet of pills restored to normal living; individuals finding a great capacity in helping other people, and that help bringing results; marriages restored; physical healing (incl. myself); churches brought to life and into dynamic and meaningful evangelism etc . . etc. . . .etc. . . .Hallelujah!'

(Blaithwaite House, Cumbria)

'We have benefited enormously, and continue to do so, by an almost astronomical rise in giving. The budget for the two Churches in 1976 was about £8,000 (£4,000 each); the budget for the two Churches for 1981 is £45,000. Income for the last two years has risen respectively by 30 per cent in 1979 and 1980, the income for 1981 is at present running at 75 per cent up on 1980. A Gift Day, the first of its kind, was held in early December 1980. Previous Gift Days had been of the sort in years gone by where the Vicar sits at the Church door and asks the passing people for money and raises usually £400-£600. We anticipated, because of the economic situation of our people and the country, a giving of £2,000-£4,000, but the gross total is now £11,000.'

(St James' and Emmanuel, Didsbury, Manchester)

'One of the benefits has been a certain open-heartedness to Christians of all labels and denominations. For instance, there was a great suspicion of the Catholic community and a considerable gulf between us some ten years ago. There is now much greater freedom in our relations with the Catholics. There is further among some a real desire for effective fellowship with local Christians from other churches.'

(St Stephen, East Twickenham)

(e) *Future Goals*
'We are deeply conscious of our call to present Jesus to the community in which we live and to bring reconciliation and unity to a multi-racial community.'

(Holy Trinity, Hounslow)

'The building of the new church centre in the new development area of the Parish, this will enable a more effective outreach to be introduced in this area.'

(Canford Magna, Dorset)

'With the change from student emphasis (we now find only 40 or 50 using us) and a greater maturity among our members, we feel ready to tackle the parish unit. Over the last ten years there has been so much to do with the crowd we have had coming to us that there has been no time for us to go to the parish. Now we know we should and there is eagerness to do so. We are seven weeks into a year's programme of study called One Step Forward — the three terms dealing with Agape, Commitment and growth, and Evangelism. This is encouraging everyone and we are full of hope, more united and altogether feeling that the pains have been birth pangs; so we are praising God for all that He has done already and for all that He is going to do in the future.'

(St Margaret, Durham)

28

(f) *Other things of note*
'As Healing Services grew and, above all, as the family of God had really become a family, and brothers and sisters were sharing their lives with each other, so we believe that the Lord was calling us to buy a large house as a Home of Healing. Miraculously, this is now functioning and is lovingly cared for by the church family. Many miracles have occurred there, and lives have been changed.'

(Holy Trinity, Littleborough, Lancs)

'It is easy to talk of success; we need to be careful that the warmth that we feel spiritually in our fellowship does not become introspective. We need also all the grace and understanding for those who are just as sincere in their discipleship of Christ but who for whatever reason do not find the new sense of adventure or enthusiasm to their liking.'

(St James' and Emmanuel, Didsbury, Manchester)

'The above alludes to various features of parish life. I am aware that it is difficult to say how far certain features should be attributed to general attention to the scriptures and how far they can be attributed to a particular movement. There seems to be now a blurring of the boundaries between the charismatic movement and wider church life. The various features of our own church life have been developed because they seem to be authentically Christian rather than because they belong to a particular movement, and it almost seems to be sufficient for any individual Christian or individual church to face the challenge of the word of God as it comes to us in many different ways.'

(St Stephen, East Twickenham)

CHAPTER 3

The Distinctive Phenomena of the Movement

The expressed intention of this report, to describe the charismatic movement, is by this stage pressing for a review of many specific areas distinctive of the movement. Not only has the historical material opened up the existence of these areas, but the parish self-descriptions have added an urgent necessity for some more integrated mapwork. The descriptions have not been standardized — they are simply as they have come from a dozen different pens — and they are not wholly amenable to being standardized! But from the history, and from these, it is possible to pick on certain items requiring more concentrated treatment.[1]

SOME GENERAL POINTS

Although the title 'charismatic' suggests an emphasis on 'gifts'[2] yet the starting-point in identifying the charismatic movement lies elsewhere — in the 'baptism in the Spirit'. The corporateness of the movement, which is important, may be slightly obscured by a treatment which begins with an individualistic experience, but there seems no doubt that historically and experimentally this experience of the individual preceded and underlay any corporate developments. From this we gain three *categories* of matters for investigation — the 'baptism', the gifts, and the subculture.

1. BAPTISM IN THE HOLY SPIRIT

We have seen that the events at Topeka, Kansas, and at Azusa Street, Los Angeles, at the beginning of the century derived from a quest for the 'baptism in the Spirit', a quest which was rewarded and a baptism which was evidenced by the 'gift of tongues'. The two — the baptism and the gift of tongues — were nearly, though not wholly, identified. Michael Harper writes:

'[In the Azusa Street blessing] On November 10th [1906] T.B. Barratt received what he now longed for — the gift of tongues — and with it a further deep experience of the Holy Spirit, *so that later he doubted whether his October experience had in fact been the Baptism in the Spirit.*' (Our italics)[3]

Thus the experience was generally reckoned to be attested through the practice of speaking in tongues, and this strand of teaching has persisted as one understanding still to be found within Pentecostalism. The underlying certainty was that the 'baptism' was a single crisis experience, a sense of being flooded, or saturated, or overcome, with God's Spirit in tremendous power. The experience has frequently been so powerful that the recipient was unable to stand, or was in other ways physically affected. When, as so often, it has been accompanied by speaking in other (and unknown) languages, it has appeared only too obvious to those experiencing it that a straight line can and should be drawn from the experience of the disciples on the day of Pentecost, or the experience of Cornelius and his household as recorded in Acts chapter 10. 'This' was surely 'that'?

The assertion does however leave certain questions unanswered; indeed it raises certain questions in a form they have not taken before in the history of the church:

(a) Is the crisis event of this 'baptism in the Spirit' always a *second* event following conversion?

(b) Is the crisis event of the 'baptism' necessary to a full Christian life in the power of the Spirit?

(c) Is the crisis event of the 'baptism' inextricably linked with the experience of speaking in tongues? If not, how can it be known that a crisis was *the* baptism? If so, why does it not always happen?

(d) Does the 'baptism' require an experienced crisis at all? Or are there ways in which people may become Pentecostal by slow change?

Whilst these questions have some parallels with the questions raised by the various holiness and 'second blessing' movements, their actual form is unique to the twentieth century.

However, they also involve a principle of interpretation on which it may be important to dwell briefly. The teaching of the 'baptism in the Spirit' is in essence a teaching that Christianity is an *experience* as much as, and more than, a *doctrine*. So the Acts of the Apostles presents it (and here J.D.G. Dunn[4] is in warm agreement with Pentecostals) and so believers experience it today. 'This' *is* 'that' — and any attempt to teach that a 'baptism' could be received without being consciously experienced is obviously going to make difficult headway against the appealing simplicity and breathtaking dynamic of the claim. Dry exegetes of scripture should beware .... To resist the claim on intellectual grounds — even on the consistency of scripture overall — is to tempt the claimant onto what is from his point of view false ground, and he rightly will not go. His experience is primary, and that is non-negotiable.

(The 'baptism in the Spirit' is the subject of a larger treatment from a scriptural standpoint in Appendix 3)

2. THE GIFTS OF THE SPIRIT

(a) The Gift of 'Tongues'

As we have noted, there is an ambivalence within Pentecostalism about the absolute necessity of the gift of 'tongues', or its inextricable identification with the baptism in the Holy Spirit. But even where it is allowed — as it generally is amongst Anglican charismatics — that this gift does not *necessarily* accompany the 'baptism', yet there is always a very high value put upon it, and a general atmosphere exists suggesting that this is highly desirable. Thus many a person who speaks in tongues has in fact first sought for the gift, prayed for it, and perhaps received a laying on of hands with a view to that end.

It is acknowledged that 'tongues' is a gift which may be exercised by an individual on his own. In such cases the non-cerebral part of a believer may have full expression towards God, the need to *frame* prayers or praises disappears, and, as those so gifted testify, there is a consequent greater freedom in the presence of God. 'Tongues' does not necessarily, nor even usually, issue in ecstasy (despite the NEB translation of *glossai* in I Corinthians as 'Ecstatic speech, the language of ecstasy'), but the person retains control over the gift, however strong the urge is to let it have full rein.[5]

However, there is a strong emphasis amongst charismatics upon the fact that 'gifts' are for the benefit of the 'Body of Christ'. It is therefore the exercise of 'tongues' in corporate worship or informal fellowship gatherings which is particularly to be noted. The same principles obtain as when the gift is exercised privately, but the New Testament principle is also noted that the use of tongues should be followed by 'interpretation' (I Cor. 14.27,28). Thus in an assembly there may well be speech in an unknown tongue, followed by prayer, praise, or exhortation (sometimes in the form of 'prophecy' — see below) in the vernacular. The relationship of the interpretation to the utterance in a tongue is usually beyond investigation, and the one who interprets will regularly say that he or she did not *understand* the utterance, but felt deeply impelled within to give what is taken to be the 'interpretation'.[6]

Charismatic literature abounds with stories of the use of a 'tongue' which was unknown to the speaker himself, but which proved to be the language of some other person present. But these, even when treasured in the memory and becoming part of folklore of the movement, are recognized as exceptional and are a kind of unforeseen bonus from the exercise of the gift. Indeed, much of the exercise of tongues has a mellifluous cadence to it unlike languages in use on earth, and it would be surprising to discover that such sounds actually were the language of other nations or people.

This gift has become almost *the* central 'recognition-symbol' for charismatics.[7] When the question is asked 'are the gifts used?', then it is almost certain that the questioner is asking 'will I hear tongues and prophecy, and perhaps witness healing, if I am present?'. And because the gift has that masonic-like 'recognition' character,[8] the actual speaking in tongues by one person has a great reassuring effect on others (particularly in a denomination like the Church of England where overall this is a rare occurrence) — a deep sense of security — 'yes, God is still with us in power'. And for the charismatic who is visiting a new church or fellowship, the sound of 'tongues' will (in this 'recognition' way) make him feel instantly at home.

('Tongues' is also the subject of more extended scriptural treatment in Appendix 4)

(b) Prophecy

'Prophecy' is joined with 'tongues' in the discussion in I Corinthians 14, and thus there is a highlighting of two of the gifts listed in I Corinthians 12. Whilst the New Testament scholars remain unsure what distinguished 'prophecy' from other utterance in the age of the apostles (and again not all the versions of the Bible even render the Greek *propheteia* as 'prophecy', so that in such versions it is difficult to pick out from the English where 'prophecy' actually comes in the original), yet there is a common practice of 'prophecy' amongst charismatics. This is distinguished from other types of exhortation by its directness — it claims to come straight from God to the recipients. Thus its grammatical form, even though uttered by a human being, is often 'I the Lord say unto you, "....".' There may be slightly less direct forms of utterance which are still treated as 'prophecy' — either introduced by a slightly more cautious note ('I wonder whether God is not saying to us "...."?'), or taking the form of describing a vision (or mental picture) or reporting a dream, from which the hearers may recognize God's word to them.[9]

'Prophecy' in general claims to be *specific*. It is God speaking to *this* gathering at this time.[10] It may be a message for all present, or for only one or two, or for those 'whom the cap fits'. And it may be exercised privately also, as one person receives from God a message for another.

There are two views to be found amongst charismatics as to the status of prophetic utterances — the more supernaturalist view, found mostly in the less perspicacious rank-and-file, being that 'prophecy' is self-authenticating, and its very directness requires unquestioning confidence and obedience (though the more cynical observer might then note that the actual 'prophecies' issued under such claims are often so general as not to be falsifiable!). The more cautious view, generally adopted by the leadership, is that 'prophecies' have to be 'tested' (I Corinthians 14.29, I Thessalonians 5.19-21). This in turn means that when 'prophecy' is exercised in the assembly, careful leadership and control is needed, lest the sheer forcefulness of utterance should lead any astray. A tension exists here.

The unquestioning enthusiast would say that every other consideration must give way when a 'prophecy' is announced, and would urge prompt acceptance and obedience. The stricter critic would point to the danger of looking too readily for instant solutions, short-cut guidance and the dangers of self-deception or group manipulation, and would urge the exercising of other gifts in order to 'test the spirits'.

'Prophecy' like 'tongues' gives to modern charismatics that comforting assurance that God is still at work in power among them, and they feel bereft if they do not regularly encounter it. (It too is the subject of more detailed treatment in Appendix 5 below.)

(c) Healing

Healing has a long and respectable history in the Christian Church, and the Anglican Churches overseas have often restored the use of anointing with oil

33

sacramentally in accordance with the teaching of the New Testament (e.g. James ch. 5), and the brief nod in that direction made by the 1549 Prayer Book. There have been in the last hundred years also both the general work of the Guild of St Raphael, and the more particular ministry of George Bennett, to enthuse different parts of the Church of England for a ministry of healing. Unlike 'tongues' and 'prophecy', healing has some actual background in Anglican practice.

However, the *mood* of healing in the Pentecostal tradition — the mood which the Charismatic movement has exhibited and promoted within the Church of England — could hardly be more polarized from previous practice than it is. Whatever the continuities with the previous cautious and rational (though caring) ministry of healing, the discontinuities are far greater. The mood which has swept in is one of expecting miracles.[11] No longer does miraculous healing need explaining — now it is non-healing which has to be explained! God is expected to be at work in power, and the spate of charismatic books of recent years fills to overflowing with the record of how God has both met and exceeded these expectations.

The ministry of healing is fulfilled amongst charismatics not only by the 'elders' (which James 5 would suggest), but also by those with a 'gift' of healing (I Cor 12.9, 28). The ministry may be exercised in public worship or privately, and is almost invariably done by prayer with the laying on of hands, often by several people. (The Eucharist has become, for many, a central focus for this ministry.) Anointing seems to have been less used by charismatics (perhaps because of the reliance on the 'gift' basis for the ministry, i.e. from I Corinthians 12-14, rather than on the 'eldership' basis, from James 5).

Healing is conceived of in very full terms, and not just physical ones, though physical healing is consciously sought, and often experienced. But the healing of the spirit (and of relationships, and of buried memories, and of conscience), along with the actual enjoyment of God's salvation, give benefits which come alongside the physical healings. They enrich the concept of healing, but also (it must be acknowledged) entail that even if no physical healing is witnessed, yet it can be confidently asserted that God has still been healing. To some observers this can look like giving God the advantage of a 'Heads-I-win-tails-you-lose' analysis of whatever happens.

An ambivalence remains at the heart of this. It takes the form of a question: 'Has God commissioned his Church to perform miracles of healing?' or, in other words, 'Can *we* say to the paralyşed man "Arise, take up your bed and walk"?'. The dilemma is that, even for very high-profile charismatics, there are not the same results as were seen in New Testament times, but to admit that, and to fall back on a ministry of healing which sounds as though it is robbed of its power and authority and certainty by a thousand qualifications in the small print, is to abandon the straight line which charismatics wish to draw from Jesus' ministry to ours. Some charismatics may answer this dilemma by saying that gifts of prophecy (or

34

'discernment', I Cor. 12.10) will enable the ministers of healing to distinguish between those who are to have physical healing, and those who are not. But even this distinguishing, while it may mean that the record of physical healing moves much closer to 100 per cent, is still far short of that 100 per cent in practice.

For the moment it is enough to acknowledge both the new emphasis upon healing and the undoubted glorious healings which have occurred, whilst noting the questions that remain.

(d) Other 'gifts'
There are other 'gifts' mentioned in the Bible, and there is a tendency for charismatics to discover and utilize these 'gifts' as a very special form of God's current revealing of himself. I Corinthians ch. 12 (for instance) in addition to those already discussed includes the 'word of wisdom', the 'word of knowledge', 'faith', the 'working of miracles', and so on.[12] So, although the phenomena of the movement have laid greatest emphasis upon 'tongues', 'prophecy' and 'healings', yet a cluster of less well advertised gifts is also to be found.

Again, it is arguable that there is an ambivalence. Are the 'gifts' in the various biblical lists an exhaustive set, or simply an illustration of the great variety of gifts? Charismatics do not always speak with the same voice on this issue — for there is a great instinct on the other hand to recognize and to employ 'gifts' of music or art (or even serving coffee or selling books), yet the great weight given to the actual practice of 'tongues' 'prophecy' and 'healing' suggests that the biblical lists have a semi-acknowledged claim to be at least normative and possibly even exhaustive of God's gifts.[13]

In every case there is an insistence that 'gifts' are for the good of the 'body', to build it up in Christ. This is a call to humility for the 'gifted' persons, and an indication of the way the 'gift' should be used. It leaves open a further question, which arises at intervals, as to whether a 'gift' is 'given' for life or for a long period, in such a way that it resides predictably with that person, or whether (to put the opposite extreme) 'gifts' only exist when they are being exercised, and the fact that one man is 'prophesying' today tell us nothing as to whether he will have that gift tomorrow — another person may be the bearer of 'prophecy' then.

3. OTHER FEATURES OF THE CHARISMATIC MOVEMENT (THE 'SUBCULTURE')
After the treatment of the 'baptism' and the 'gifts' we find a whole plethora of characteristics which help to identify charismatics, but which are not so specifically drawn from scriptural terminology. It is these which we have earlier dubbed the 'subculture'. Cumulatively they add strongly to the 'masonic-like recognition-symbols' also mentioned earlier.

(a) In worship
Charismatics aim at a distinctive *style* of worship. It can be argued that it is simply an extension of the course which the Liturgical Movement was steering in any case — but it must be admitted that, if so, it is often a very

35

far-reaching extension. The freedom desired and experienced goes light-years beyond the gentle loosening up and relaxing which the Liturgical Movement has brought. We may specify some of these characteristics as follows:

(i) There is a thoroughgoing *use of the body*. Hands may be lifted into the air in praise (or extended palm upwards in adoration or supplication), hands may be laid on each other in prayer, arms may be linked during corporate singing (and bodies may sway sensuously in time with the music), the kiss of peace may involve an extensive hug-in, feet may tap, hands may clap, and individuals may dance. The 1978 conference at Canterbury before the Lambeth Conference became famous for the dance of the bishops round the main communion table in Canterbury Cathedral at the close of a three-hour eucharist — a dance preserved for history not only as a vivid memory amongst those who were present, but also caught by the camera and printed on the cover of *A New Canterbury Tale*.[14] Yes, bodies were well involved. In addition, there is wide use of drama, dance drama, and mime. Bodies are vehicles for ministering to each other the love of Christ, and they sometimes may be used freely in these ways.

(ii) There are new styles of *music*. A creative talent has been unleashed, and all and sundry now write their praises and their prayers to be sung as new songs. *Sound of Living Waters* (1974) and *Fresh Sounds* (1976) have already been mentioned. The guitar has become central to the musical culture, and praise has overtaken cerebral content to give a new mood to corporate singing.[15] At the same time, the new song books do have sections devoted to 'liturgical songs', and the scriptural, liturgical and sacramental emphases have not been overlooked.

Singing has gained not only a new involvement of the body, new instruments, and new words — it is also used in new informal ways. Times of prayer may be punctuated by the suggesting or leading off of a well-known song or chorus, and open times (such as during the administration of communion) may be used for a very gentle singing, or alternatively for a mounting climax of full-throated song. Whilst these moods may be led or set by key persons, they can in fact feel to the participants as though they are being taken over by a power of God, greater than themselves. The ultimate stage of this is the corporate activity known as 'singing in tongues' where whole congregations strike off into wordless musical notes and rhythms, not in *time* with each other but in a marvellous unity-in-diversity with each other. Guitarists and other instrumentalists can both introduce and reinforce this practice.

(iii) There is a *freedom* for contributions, for personal devotion, for singing and for seeking counselling. This goes far beyond the traditional evangelical extempore prayer meeting, because of the range of activities which the freedom incorporates. As shown in connection with 'prophecy', it also requires very clear leadership. And a most interesting feature of charismatic worship has been the ministry of not only 'healing' but also prayer with the laying on of hands, and many forms of counselling *within* public worship —

often after people have received communion, but also during the intercessions.

(iv) A feature of charismatic worship is the *rally*. Special meetings — e.g. midweek ones with a special speaker, are used not so much for the preaching (though that may be there), but for the experience of corporate worship on a large-scale. This may in particular be a time for praise and joy, a leading upwards from ordinary experience into a widely shared jubilant worship of a God who is known in power.

(v) Underneath the covert feature of charismatic worship there has developed what Colin Buchanan calls an *'inchoate sacramentality'*[16] — bodies, music, artwork, movement, colour, the sacraments themselves — these all conspire to inculcate a positive sacramentalism even amongst those who had previously been non-sacramentalist, or even anti-sacramentalist, and those with a sacramental tradition testify that this has been greatly enhanced. As with so many other features of this renewal, this change comes not through good argument driving out bad, but by new contagious practice infecting the practitioners with new 'gut-level' understanding of the created order and its role in our approach to God and his to us.

(b) In structures
(i) An over-simplistic interpretation of the New Testament emphases on the local, permanent and supervisory nature of 'eldership' has led to a widespread notion of *'lay elders'*. In places this has issued in a desire to *add* this element to Anglican structures of, e.g., vicar, curate, lay reader, wardens and PCC. It is often easier to add such an office than it is to define its powers and responsibilities over against existing offices. Nevertheless the attempt is being constantly made, and may well give added impetus to the Church of England to review its structure of local ministry.[17]

(ii) With the charismatic movement, and probably because of it, there has arisen a greater desire for *'pastoring'*. On analysis this may prove to be a desire for a dependent-relationship, for directive forms of spiritual oversight. Where this is particularly strongly felt or experienced, then there is also a tug in the direction of the House Church Movement, where a more highly developed pattern of oversight exists, arguably tighter and closer in its execution than any form of oversight in the Church of God ought to be. We note that in some places there is a fiercely hierarchical character to that Movement, compared with which the Church of England appears almost indifferent to the ordering of spiritual oversight. (See Appendix 6.)

(c) In 'Spiritual Warfare'
Another great phenomenon of the charismatic movement has been the renewed awareness of the demonic, and with it an exercising of 'deliverance' ministries. As with healing, the matter is not new — but, as with healing, the *mood* has been revolutionized. Partly, there seems in some to be an actual *desire* to discern the invasion of the devil. Partly, there has been a corresponding increase in exorcism, including lay and instant exorcism. Partly, there have been some stupendous deliverances, increasing

the amazed sense that God is working in great power among us, and through us. Partly, the demonic has been widely overlooked or forgotten in the Church in the last century and a half.[18] But, whatever the reasons, the movement at large has witnessed a sense that we 'wrestle .... against principalities and powers ....' — with men and women giving themselves to that wrestling with a crusading and committed spirit. We are conscious, however, that this is one of the areas which has raised the greatest doubts and anxieties, both over the incautious practising of exorcism, and, for some, about the whole theology underlying it.

(d) In Biblical Interpretation
From one point of view the charismatic movement is a form of Christian existentialism. Above all, God is alive and well, and is meeting with us, teaching us, leading us — NOW! If people have been delivered from the dryness of their previous experience, and given the refreshing and life-conveying 'baptism in the Spirit', then their present experience is crucial to them. In their use of the Bible they may step back one pace or so from where the more intellectually orientated Christian scholarship of today would want them to go. Thus the Bible's chief use may be not to testify to the history of God's dealings with his people, not to establish general principles, but rather to give direct messages and direct guidance today. Scripture will be laid under contribution in 'prophecy' and in counselling without regard to context, but only with regard to some course of action which the handling of the text in a particular way may further. Texts are turned into song on a similar basis. The severe critic would want to suggest that this method of procedure means that all norms of doctrine and practice become frail. Once anything can mean anything, then the movement becomes afloat on a sea of subjectivism. And there is always a tendency in that direction. It is, for instance, arguable that some charismatics, for all their address to the Son and to the Spirit, are only Trinitarian by *accident* — they happen to have gained their new and normative *experience of* God within a Trinitarian tradition, so that the tradition has moulded their expression of their faith (as in hymns with three verses addressed to Father, Son, and Holy Spirit!), when the experience of itself could not and would not have so determined it.

By contrast, others have initially thought themselves to be caught up in a Jesus-cult or a Spirit-cult, but have found this to be the doorway to a real *experience* of the Triune God, whereas previously they had only given lip service to a somewhat incomprehensible trinitarian theology. And yet others believe themselves to have had their eyes opened to the dimensions of biblical theology and especially Semitic philosophy through this movement which call them to a very radical reappraisal of the whole Trinitarian formulation of Christian doctrine. The point therefore remains that, if experience is made the chief arbiter of understanding, then certitudes based on tradition and doctrine are no longer secure. (For some this is liberation indeed!)

38

(e) Cross-fertilization

It is likely that the charismatic movement brings missing dimensions to some of the existing traditions in the church. To the evangelical, it brings a release from negative attitudes to sacramentalism, and the created order. Cartoon puritanism is swept aside, and a healthy reform of worship is set in hand. The evangelical may also be delivered from his fear of Rome, and thus share in worship and activities with Roman Catholic charismatics, on a basis of true mutual acceptance rather than fierce hostility.

To the radical or 'social-activist' Anglican, the movement has brought a new sense of the luminous reality of God, and the centrality of worship.

To the Catholic (whether Anglican or Roman) the movement has often brought the Bible to life. It has broken its formal and liturgical bounds, and come into the life of the congregation and individual with a vividness and power which has astonished the recipients.

On the other hand, the critic is still free to say that charismatics duck the harder intellectual tasks of Christian discipleship . . . .

(f) Love and openness

The importance of the corporate has already emerged a dozen times over. But it is no mechanical rearrangement of relations which interests charismatics. They believe in *love*. Hence the embracing. Hence the freedom with each other. Hence the sustained prayer for each other. There *is* new love. On the other hand, this may appear to the outsider as mere cosiness, corporate navel-gazing. And do the like gravitate to the like, or is there a genuine growth of love between the unlike? (One element that encourages a more positive response to this last question is the way that so many inadequate and emotionally crippled people are being tended within this movement, as the accounts at the end of Chapter 2 bear witness.)

(g) Romanticism?

Here we are going beyond the phenomena into causality. But one common bond of all the items above is the air of romanticism with which Church life is invested. This may express itself in the love of the miraculous, or in anti-intellectualism, or in many other ways. Such a mood has always accompanied a reaction to 'classicalism' (see Chapter 4 section 4). But inspection will suggest that it *is* a common bond, and contact with charismatics will usually confirm this. But then, perhaps Christianity itself *must* have an element of romanticism to be Christianity worthy of the name?

It is perhaps to the romanticism of the movement that various other 'subcultural' activities can be attributed. Community living may or may not qualify. Creativity — even third rate creativity, though much of it is well above third-rate — does so qualify. The pursuit of cottage industries, usually of the 'zany arts and crafts' variety, is surely due to romanticism? And it is not difficult to read back the same common precipitating factor into much of the rest of the subculture.

CHAPTER 4

What gave rise to the Movement in the Church of England?

The question which heads this chapter invites the simple answer 'God — and God alone'.[1] However a working group which accepted that answer simplistically without any qualification or further question would be unable to report in the way that the original synod motion required, and would in fact be failing the charismatics themselves. For if the charismatic renewal of the 1960s and 1970s be attributed wholly to God, yet we are left with consequential questions arising: 'Why did God do that *at this moment in time?*' 'What casual links did God use to bring it about?' and so on. And if there is some doubt as to the God-given character of the movement, then all the more we are left to investigate what factors within the life of the Church gave rise to it. We suggest half a dozen factors of differing weight and heterogeneous character which may assist in any evaluation.

1. THE ACTS OF THE APOSTLES?

No amount of sterilization of the biblical message, and no amount of critical scholarship, have ever managed wholly to conceal the flow of the Acts narrative, and its message of a Spirit-filled community facing persecution, working miracles, rejoicing in the power of God, and generally living a corporate 'Pentecostal' life. The challenge is there — and the Church has always writhed slightly uneasily in trying to diminish the challenge. The alternative response — to rise to the challenge and to attempt to live a comparable corporate life — inevitably presses itself upon us. And the charismatic movement has undoubtedly tried thus to rise to the challenge. If the result is a different pattern of Church life, then the reason might well be because so much of inherited Anglicanism has been busy *evading* that challenge. Yet still the question haunts us — is there not a freedom, a joyfulness, a carefreeness, a dimension of living in the Spirit, a glad self-surrender, an overflowing love, which no amount of insistence on decency and good order will ever quite supply? The Liturgical Movement might conceivably point in this direction (from far off), but little else in the Church of England in the twentieth or indeed the preceding centuries has given any encouragement to this development. It is the witness of Acts to which we trace back the impetus.

2. A MISSING EXPERIENCE?

We have previously emphasized the experiential character of the charismatic movement — and indeed of the charismatic phenomena. Is there something authentic to be *experienced* which traditional mainstream Church life has obscured — something authentic to being children of God

40

and humankind in the presence of God?[2] Is it possible that an institutionalized, intellectualized, formalized (and even fossilized) practice of Christianity has left a thirst in the inner being which only the springs of charismatic renewal could satisfy? Is it a renewed supernaturalism, a renewed sense of *seeing and feeling* God at work, which the Church at large has been missing? It is only too believable.

3. A REACTION AGAINST CLERICALISM?

Clericalism is the inevitable legacy of the medieval and reformation eras. Until the nineteenth century, none but the clergyman could as much as read a lesson in Church, and the main lay officers — the churchwardens — had no spiritual leadership, no liturgical responsibility, no pastoral role, to fulfil. The clergyman *was* the church, when anything in these areas had to be done, and the 'rediscovery of the laity' has generally been happening faster in works of theology than it has been doing on the ground (with some honourable exceptions).[3] Indeed, it is arguable that the rise of Anglo-catholicism, with its augmented notions of the 'priesthood' and 'apostolic descent' and 'indelible character' of the ordained ministry, actually delayed this 'rediscovery' by a century or more. Evangelicals too, for all that they pay more lip-service to the active role of the laity, have so often proved clericalist in their practice. And Christians who exhibit natural (let alone supernatural!) gifts in their secular callings have often felt cramped when confined to giving out hymnbooks or arranging flowers as their sole contribution to the life of the Church. Thus, there has been in this century an inarticulate, unformed, unreflective pool of spiritual energies waiting to be used by the Church, but not well tapped or laid under contribution by the general patterns of Anglican parish life. Perhaps a movement emphasising 'every member ministry' has released this pool of energies. Again, others have been moving in this direction, but the charismatic movement has overtaken such others by the sheer speed with which it has brought change.

4. AN EXISTENTIALIST ATMOSPHERE?

The rise of an existentialist atmosphere in many secular circles in recent decades is a matter of fact. The causes of this are not our present task to trace out. But whether it is the effect of living with the bomb (where the future has no reality which can be faced), or the result of a decline in the old 'classical education' (which, on the one hand, traditionally preserved a sense of history, and sequence, and cause and effect, and moral responsibility — but, on the other, may have been largely responsible for preserving the inordinate primacy of the 'cerebral' over the 'spiritual' so evident in the western world) or simply the surfacing of an attitude which is natural to fallen man but has previously been checked by the values of Christendom — these questions need not detain us. The fact is certain. And it is arguable that the charismatic movement reflects a form of Christianised existentialism. The emphasis on *experience* is a centring on the present, the current, the ephemeral. A culture which majors on 'testimony' might be viewed as a culture which offered an alternative 'trip' — a Jesus 'trip' — to a generation already prone to an acid or drugs 'trip'. Charismatics are certainly open at points to this altered gospel, and, if any persist in cutting historical and intellectual corners, they may imbibe it and make it their own — their norm. It would be hard to show that there has been a direct causal link, but the secular and the charismatic trends have moved synchronously, and the less satisfactory expressions of the charismatic movement look remarkably like a Christianised existentialism. If there is a seed of the rise of the movement in this, then there is also some cause for alarm. The gospel can easily become 'another gospel', where although the credal statements may continue to appear in the hymnody, they appear to be without historical grounding, and their affirmatory character diminishes to vanishing point.

5. A RELIEF FROM FORMALISM?

With the rise of existentialism has come a strong reaction against formalism. The features of charismatic worship noted above represent an escape from the 'stately masked ball' of traditional Anglican worship — the masks are shed, the people seen, the carefully rehearsed and executed slow steps are abandoned for a quicker rhythm, and the stateliness is lost in the dawning of the real and authentic. Anglican formalism lived by a liturgical rule-book — you bow here, stand silent there, gaze to the front throughout, and never relax your composure. But many people with the stirrings of a love for Christ in their hearts, and energies to sing and participate in their bodies, have longed for the escape into a greater reality — and the new movement has met them at their point of need. They are free — free to interject their 'Hallelujahs' in the prayers, free to offer their own contributions in times of open ministry, free to express themselves to each other. And, curiously and marvellously, the alternative modern-language services in the Church of England actually encourage congregations to find their own level in these ways, and have their own role to play in the escape from formalism.

6. AN IMPOVERISHED PNEUMATOLOGY?

It has been long recognized that Pneumatology, the Church's teaching about the Holy Spirit, has been an under-developed (and sometimes confusing) aspect of western theology. We are left wondering whether the partial intellectual vacuum in this area of doctrine has permitted new growth here, whereas in the more ordered areas of Christology, Ecclesiology or Soteriology for instance, it has been much easier to regulate, or even stifle, any sign of unintended shoots. It seems possible that renewed ecumenical contact with the Orthodox, as well as with classical Pentecostalism, has highlighted the impoverished pneumatology of much contemporary western theology, and the consequent lack of 'expectancy' in many ordinary church members.

None of these possible 'causes' of the charismatic movement can be offered as more than an intelligent guess, and none of them is exclusive of the others. Indeed, it should be added, none of them is exclusive of the hand of God either. For he works mysteriously, bringing his own will to pass through the good and the ill and the morally neutral of the ways of men and women. So, it might well be that all six of the suggestions above have had their part to play in the earthly causality.

CHAPTER 5
Evaluation

To establish some secondary causes, even though they be causes through which God may himself have been at work in some special way, does not *of itself* establish the movement as a special outpouring of God's power. Yet the character of those 'causes' does suggest that the charismatic movement has found itself filling a gap in traditional Anglican Christianity. (This does not of course deny that this gap may have appeared before, possibly in some other form, and been met to a greater or lesser extent by other movements e.g. evangelical pietism or Anglo-catholic spirituality). Of course the need could be truly there and yet the charismatic movement be a false solution, or the 'need' could be spurious and yet the movement have supplied something valuable and God-given. The quest for evaluation is bound to run into subjective judgements about these matters, and it is hardly a suitable issue for a majority and minority vote!

However, if we place the charismatic movement on the world-scene, and note how it has affected Churches from Rome right through to the House Church Movement, then a question starts to emerge: was Newbigin right, in *The Household of God,* to make Pentecostalism a 'third strand' in the character of the world-wide church, seen in its ideal state? And if he was right, then is the outpouring we have seen, in the very years since he wrote, a kind of fulfilment and confirmation of what he wrote? Thus the three strands would be — the 'form' of the church (catholicism), the primacy of the word (protestantism), and the experience of the Spirit (Pentecostalism). But the oddity which Newbigin did not foretell (though his whole argument points ideally towards it) is that the pentecostal experience has been found *within* the catholic and protestant traditions, and not just complementing them from the outside.

If we accept Newbigin's argument, then we have a framework of thought with which to return to the Church of England's own charismatic movement. Is it not likely that a Church which has for so long claimed to be unashamedly both catholic and protestant will also need to find a place for this 'third strand'? Its internal ecumenicity calls for this, but not only calls for it, it has got it! The Church of England claims to be catholic in the sense of being primitive and comprehensive, and disclaims being a denomination, if 'denomination' entails only a partial view of the truth of the Gospel or the nature of the Church. It must surely then recognise and welcome this pentecostal strand which has arisen so astonishingly within its own ordered and institutional life.

Though such an argument may sound fine in a Synod report, it could infuriate some charismatics! Those who are seized of a strong conviction of truth (whether Anglo-catholic or evangelical, radical or charismatic) do not take kindly to being 'patronised' with phrases like 'a valuable contribution', as though above and beyond the differing traditions within the Church of

44

England there were some super-managers, seeing themselves as above the traditions and engaged in blending them into 'the best mix'. The heirs of the Evangelical Revival and of the Oxford Movement both already know the sterilising effect of such an attitude, for to them it implies that a particular strand of tradition is but a good 'one-eyed' view, needing to be complemented by others in order to become 'two-eyed', thus denying their claim that their tradition *is* already 'two-eyed'. By the same token a charismatic may be unhappy to the point of desperation if he is only to be tolerated and included in a comprehensive Anglican bundle, and denied all chance of making a distinctive challenge that *this* (his experience) is *that* (the apostolic experience) and that he who would practise full-orbed Christianity ought to possess it.[1]

This situation presents to many Christians a major dilemma: they recognise in charismatics a new quality of joy and release yet, *with integrity,* they cannot accept much that the charismatic believes and does, (much less the uncompromising demand expressed by a few, that they themselves act likewise). It is this dilemma that underlies much tension and unhappiness in parishes where non-charismatics may experience rejection or the charismatics feel they are not accepted.

Is there a way out of this? An acceptance of the pentecostal strand that is neither patronising nor capitulation? Surely there is but it will involve long, hard and frank dialogue (of the kind that lay behind the catholic-evangelical book *Growing into Union,* 1970 or the evangelical-charismatic statement *Gospel and Spirit,* 1977). It is this kind of dialogue which we began to experience at the Ely Consultation[2] and have tried to develop in the working group, but we would be the first to say that there is still a long way to go. The essence of such dialogue is that the participants come out from their entrenched positions, become open to each other and discover not so much that they have been missing vital elements, (though they *may* discover this), but that the elements of Christianity that others are pressing on them are in fact already in their own tradition, though often forgotten or overlaid.

We cannot say how far such serious dialogue would take us. But we do see that there are certain questions which it would inevitably provoke. We set out some of them for consideration:

(a) Has something of New Testament Christianity been missing from the Church of England's life, something to which the charismatic movement bears witness?

(b) Does the breath of new life in a parish which charismatic renewal represents have to produce divisive results? If so, is the cost of renewal too high?

(c) Does the charismatic movement, with its particular preoccupations, involve a withdrawal from the social witness of the Church? It is not sufficient for charismatics to point to one or two notable African or Latin-American exceptions. We think that a more *local* answer is needed in

England. We are glad to see some contra-indications in the parish reports already cited.

(d) Is it possible that the *distinctive* character of the charismatic movement is already past its peak? If so, it may be because the 'behavioural gap' has narrowed *from the non-charismatic side.* In other words, there are now not only many parishes in a 'second generation' stage, where the instinct to the most distinctive features (whether 'tongues' or 'prophecy' or whatever) has been modified by later experience and reflection, but there are also many non-charismatic parishes feeling their way to a greater openness, a deeper experience of the Spirit, an 'every member ministry', and other features characteristic of the movement. Thus the gap has narrowed at the level of 'phenomena'. But this is without prejudice to the outbreak of charismatic renewal in further 'first generation' parishes. This still continues, and in such parishes it all seems very distinctive.

(e) Is not any evaluation we make made from within the changing times, and therefore very provisional? (And this question calls for the answer 'yes'.)

CHAPTER 6

Learning and Living Together

The writing of this report has led us in the main to welcome the charismatic movement, along with some hesitations about certain features (whether exegetical, experiential, or behavioural) of the way the movement has exhibited itself. In this chapter we have to anticipate some of the work of dialogue which we have recommeded in chapter 5, and see what mutual lessons are to be learned.

We believe that *contact and dialogue between charismatics and others has been slow to arise, for many reasons* of which the following at least are obvious:

(a) There is often a past experience of divisiveness, with past hurts still affecting present relationships.

(b) Parochial (and party) insularities mean that many Anglicans are remarkably incurious about how the other five-sixths live.

(c) Charismatics in both their public utterances and their printed books have tended to be incautious about their language (which misleads their hearers and readers), and non-charismatics have often been too stuck in more traditional modes of discourse to be able to 'hear' what is being said.

(d) Very little literature in the Church of England has been given to mutual interpretation.

(e) Actual 'excesses' do continue (as does actual 'aridity'), and there can be new polarizations for reasons of substance and not mere presentation.

However, we anticipate that, if these difficulties can be overcome, there are *powerful lessons for the rest of the Church of England to learn from the charismatic movement.* The following have in some cases arisen above, in passing, and in others are newly stated here:

(a) It is important that believers should experience the sheer reality of God, and should allow a role for such experience in private devotion and public worship.

(b) It is important that scope should exist in corporate worship for individual contributions.

(c) It is important that all Christians should be more open to each other — in small groups, in 'prayer-counselling', in the ministry of healing, and in all forms of sharing of themselves with each other. And this openness needs to be extended on all sides, and to include those who differ.

(d) It is important for the Church to release and use those gifts of creativity — in music, drama, dance, art, and writing, for instance — in worship and other areas of church life.

(e) It is important that the practical ecumenism of charismatics — a joining on the basis of a common experience and common outlook — should be cultivated by the Church of England. Of course doctrinal and confessional questions should not be ducked, but approaches to both Roman Catholics and to, say, West Indian Pentecostals on the basis of a common outlook can lead to a more fruitful dialogue about truth.

(f) Within all these other matters, there are important questions about the transcendence and the immediacy of God, which the charismatic experience has precipitated in a new way. In particular there is a need for the whole Church, nationally and locally, to exhibit a much greater 'openness' to God — so that he can do with us what he wills.

At the same time the dialogue includes *some points which non-charismatics must urge upon charismatics:*

(a) There is a need to hold on to the tension between giving special value to *this* experience and honouring the experience of others.

(b) There is a need for a greater theological concern. It has to include the integration of Bible and tradition with current experience, and thus establish both methodology and content for charismatic theology. It is only too easily arguable that a flow of instant testimony is not a substitute.

(c) In particular there is a need for some to take seriously the plea for a return to a more rounded 'Trinitarianism', however modified or enhanced this may be.[1]

And as the dialogue progresses, there are *some big questions for all to face together:*

(a) What is Christian maturity?[2]

(b) What room should a truly catholic church have for new movements, and how should it evaluate them?

(c) How do Christians learn from each other?

(d) Have we a need for a more defined Anglican stance in spirituality, in faith, and in pastoral theology? To be 'Anglican' these would have to be more than partisan, and yet without loss of sight of the particularities within the Church of England. We have come to consider that the Standing Committee might well commission more work in this area from the relevant Board or Council.

We end by saying that we have greatly enjoyed our work together on this report and have been mutually helped and blessed by it. It is our conclusion that the institution we serve *needs* to assimilate (albeit critically) many of the insights of this movement that we have examined, if it is to fulfil its part in the mission of the universal church of Jesus Christ with maximum effectiveness; but also that the exponents of this movement need the ordering and disciplining of their enthusiasm which the institution can and does provide, and which alone will preserve for the good of all, and to the glory of God, the benefits of every new outpouring of his Spirit.

Notes

CHAPTER 1

[1] The Greek word means 'free gifts'. It is used chiefly of the Holy Spirit's endowments. (See especially 1 Corinthians 12.)

[2] *Report of the Consultation on the value of charismatic renewal* held at London Colney in December 1978. (BCC, London) pp. 3-4.

[3] Liturgical Press, Collegeville, Minnesota, U.S.A., 1980

CHAPTER 2

[1] Eastern Christianity has taken another course. Its distinctive doctrines of the Spirit pose quite different questions, but it has managed to contain the 'charismatic' much more successfully. The *staretzi* of Russian Orthodoxy are a prime example of 'establishment' charismatics.

[2] Only the friars, and monasticism in some of its aspects, proved capable of sustaining an acceptable *modus vivendi* in the Church for these elements.

[3] The ministry of Edward Irving, a Scottish Presbyterian, led to the formation of the Catholic Apostolic Church in the 1830s.

[4] *A Theology of the Holy Spirit.* (Eerdmans, 1971) p. 42.

[5] For further details, see J. Root, *Encountering Westindian Pentecostalism* (Grove Books, Nottingham, 1979) pp. 4. ff.

[6] Although, as the author himself acknowledges in his foreword, this analysis owes little to the Eastern Orthodox experience.

[7] See page 7.

[8] A South African Pentecostalist who has become known as 'Mr Pentecost'.

[9] It is also reported that the Rev. John Hope, in the Diocese of Sydney, had, with others, experienced 'speaking in tongues' in the mid 1950s.

[10] A very influential 'convert' was the Rev. Graham Pulkingham of Houston, Texas, latterly Provost of Cumbrae, Scotland.

[11] C. O. Buchanan, G. D. Leonard, E. L. Mascall and J. I. Packer (pub. SPCK 1970).

[12] Also about this time, Leslie Davison, a leading British Methodist, was having a considerable influence through his identification with the movement.

[13] Hodder 1974.

[14] By Michael Harper, Hodder 1979.

[15] Reproduced in *The Churchman* April 1977.

[16] See Chapter 1, footnote 2.

[17] Indeed, regular gatherings for 'Praise and Prayer' — a marked feature of 'charismatic' worship — now take place early each morning in Church House when Synod is in session.

[18] There have, for instance, been occasional services in Cathedrals (Guildford, Lincoln, Canterbury, St Paul's) which have provided an openness for liturgical expression very much in the 'charismatic' mould.

[19] *Renewal* Magazine, edited by Michael Harper, is being published by Edward England. (12 Highlands Close, Crowborough, East Sussex.)

The journal, *Theological Renewal,* edited by Tom Smail is being published by Grove Books. (St John's College, Bramcote, Nottingham.)
The *Fountain Trust books* are obtainable from Christian Literature Crusade. (The Dean, Alresford, Hampshire.)
The *Fountain Trust tapes* are obtainable from Renewal Servicing (P.O. Box 366, Addlestone, Weybridge, Surrey) and from St John's College.

CHAPTER 3

[1] We recognize that there are some who question the whole enterprise of an analytical and systematic approach to describing the charismatic movement, and we especially sympathize with those who liken this to 'digging up the potatoes to see if they are growing'! Nevertheless, whilst admitting the inevitable inadequacy of our endeavours, we are persuaded that the attempt should be made.

[2] See page 1.

[3] *As at the Beginning* p. 30.

[4] See page 8.

[5] We do not, by saying this, wish to denigrate 'ecstasy' in any way, nor to deny that ecstasy *may* accompany speaking in tongues. We are simply recording that 'speaking in tongues' and 'ecstasy' are *not* co-terminous or interdependent.

[6] Part of the problem is that, in the N.T., the word *hermeneuo* and its compounds may equally well mean 'translate' *or* 'interpret'. It has a prior meaning of 'explain'.

[7] One of our most respected correspondents insists that this phase is now past, and that this is no longer so central as it was.

[8] We are asked to point out, in using the analogy of 'masonic' symbols, that Charismatics on the whole are passionately *opposed* to free-masonry.

[9] cf., e.g, ed. Michael Harper, *A New Canterbury Tale* (Grove Books. 1978) p.32.

[10] Some would therefore question the propriety of writing down such 'prophecies' and passing them around, as if they had a more universal significance.

[11] We detect a marked contrast in this movement between some who see 'miracles' in what has been termed a super-supernaturalist way i.e. evidencing the dramatic, direct finger of a strongly interventionist God, and those who regard things like healing, deliverance from unclean spirits etc. as a wholly *natural* activity, a restoring of order and normality and a sign of God's ordinary activity in his world, and who would even suggest that the word 'miracle', with its latinized connotations, is itself unhelpful in this context.

[12] Romans ch. 12 and Ephesians ch. 4 have other lists that differ in some details.

[13] Ever here, though, we note in some a tendency to discriminate, with (say) 'teaching' or 'administration' sometimes getting much too low a rating!

[14] See pages 11 and 33. These, it will be remembered were *Anglican* (though *not* Church of England!) bishops. We should point out that this occasion was also marked by a deep awareness that some of those present faced great trials on their return home, and that their inordinate 'joy' was preceded by a perhaps inordinate 'weeping'.

[15] This new music varies enormously in quality when gauged by traditional critique. Some has proved extremely ephemeral, some serves only mantra-like purposes (achieved by 'hypnotic' repetition), but some will no doubt endure and become classic.

[16] In *Encountering Charismatic Worship*. Grove Books (Nottingham) 1977. p. 19.

[17] For some this raises much wider issues of 'authority' — see, e.g., Rex Davis in *Locusts and Wild Honey* (WCC 1978) pp. 94, 95.

[18] Indeed some would go so far as to argue that this aspect ought not to be dealt with under the heading of 'sub-culture' at all, but that the movement's involvement in this marks the recovery of a 'holistic' gospel thrust that rehabilitates the classical trio of preaching, healing and deliverance from unclean spirits (as found, e.g., in Matt. 4.23,24 and, especially, Matt. 10.5-8).

CHAPTER 4

[1]It may be noted here that those caught up in this movement show a marked preference for the more devotional 'covenant' designation 'The Lord', rather than the general appellation 'God', when speaking of the Divinity.

[2]Though we suspect this is that same spiritual authenticity to which the mystics and contemplatives have so long pointed.

[3]We refer partly to the ministry of Sunday School teachers, youth leaders and those in women's ministry — though even here the clerical hand has usually been heavy and dominating.

CHAPTER 5

[1] Though, at the Ely Consultation (see Appendix 2), John Richards said of *his* assessment, from within the Charismatic movement, of what it should contribute to the Church, 'Mint sauce should be assessed by what it does for the lamb!'

[2]See Appendix 2.

CHAPTER 6

[1] Though we also recognize the force of the argument of some charismatics that, if the mainstream churches had themselves exhibited 'a more rounded Trinitarianism', including an adequate theology of the Holy Spirit, the 'rediscovery' of the distinctives of the Movement would have been quite unnecessary!

[2] This subject is opened up in a helpful way in an essay, 'Christian Maturing', by Michael Harper in Vol, 1. of the papers prepared for the 1977 National Evangelical Anglican Congress, entitled *Obeying Christ in a Changing World* (Fountain, 1977).

Bibliography

The principal works alluded to in the report are as follows.
Those marked * contain further useful bibliographical material.

Dennis Bennett: *Nine O'clock in the Morning.* Coverdale (USA) 1970

* F. Dale Bruner: *A Theology of the Holy Spirit.* Eerdmans (USA) 1971.

C. O. Buchanan: *Encountering Charismatic Worship.* Grove (Nottingham) 1977

C. O. Buchanan, G. D. Leonard, E. L. Mascall, J. I. Packer: *Growing into Union.* SPCK (London) 1970

* Rex Davis: *Locusts and Wild Honey.* WCC (Geneva) 1978.

* J. D. G. Dunn: *Baptism in the Holy Spirit.* SCM (London) 1970

Fountain Trust/Church of England Evangelical Council report: *Gospel and Spirit,* published in *The Churchman* April 1977.

John Gunstone: *Greater things than these.* Faith Press (London) 1971.

(ed.) Michael Harper: *A New Canterbury Tale.* Grove (Nottingham) 1978.

Michael Harper: *As at the beginning.* Hodder (London) 1965.

Michael Harper: *Bishop's Move.* Hodder (London) 1979.

* Walter Hollenweger: *The Pentecostals.* (ET) SCM (London) 1972.

* Kilian McDonnell: *Presence, Power, Praise.* 3 vols. Liturgical Press (USA) 1980.

Lesslie Newbigin: *The Household of God.* SCM (London) 1953.

* John Root: *Encountering Westindian Pentecostalism.* Grove (Nottingham) 1979.

Colin Urquhart: *When the Spirit Comes.* Hodder (London) 1974.

Tom Walker: *Open to God: A Parish in Renewal.* Grove (Nottingham) 1975.

David Watson: *One in the Spirit.* Hodder (London) 1973.

An Account of the General Synod's Involvement

The Charismatic Movement, by its very nature, did not find its way easily onto the agenda of the General Synod. It does not fall within the Synod's normal business, nor is it immediately identifiable as within the province of a particular Board or Council, since it clearly has implications for all.

THE PRIESTNALL MOTION

The movement was probably first in view in the private member's motion tabled in November 1975 by the Rev. R. H. Priestnall (Peterborough):

'That this Synod calls upon the bishops, clergy and laity of the provinces of Canterbury and York to pray for *the renewal of the* whole *Church* in our country *in the power of the Holy Spirit,* and to reshape their worship, witness and work, so that the glory of the Lord and his salvation in Christ Jesus may be more deeply known and more clearly manifested in the lives of his people.' (Our italics.)

In February 1977 it occasioned only a short debate in a poorly attended Friday afternoon session. Perhaps because it was vague about the meaning of 'renewal', and centred on a call to prayer, the passing of the motion led to no specific action.

THE BUCHANAN MOTION

In July 1976 the Rev. C. O. Buchanan (Southwell) had tabled a private motion calling for a report on the Charismatic Movement within the Church of England. (For text see the Foreword to this report.)

Though it quickly obtained the necessary support, it had to be withdrawn as the proposer was abroad when it was due for debate, and it was tabled again. Eventually, in July 1978, in the final ten minutes one evening, Colin Buchanan made his opening speech. When the debate was resumed in November, the Bishop of Pontefract took up the matter, and a wide-ranging debate in a fairly full house took place, notable for some impassioned criticism of the movement, which elicited refutations and positive responses from a variety of positions. The Standing Committee tabled an amendment to remove the necessity for a report:

'*Leave out* all words after "Many" in line 3 down to "and" in line 6 and *insert:*
"churches, warmly commends the contribution already made by Professor Hollenweger, the Fountain Trust and the British Council of Churches amongst others to the evaluation of its particular distinctive features, and would welcome further studies which would"'.'

The proposer of the main motion stressed the importance of retaining his request for a report and, the amendment having been narrowly defeated, the original motion was passed unamended.

Meanwhile, the British Council of Churches and the Fountain Trust had convened a consultation to discuss the value of the charismatic renewal, at London Colney, Hertfordshire, in December 1978, to which representatives of the General Synod were invited along with other Anglicans. They reported on the General Synod's motion, and were encouraged to pursue the matter as expeditiously as possible.

THE ELY CONSULTATION

Accordingly the Standing Committee convened a *Consultation on Charismatic Renewal in the Church of England* at Bishop Woodford House, Ely, on 9th-10th October 1979, to give consideration to the General Synod's motion. The participants, who included both those who were, and those who were not directly involved in Charismatic renewal, were:

Chairman: The Rt Rev. Colin James, Bishop of Wakefield

Church of England Representatives:

Dr Bill Allchin
* Ven. Arthur Attwell
* Rev. Colin Buchanan
* Mr Tony Bush
* Mr James Cobban
* Canon Colin Craston
  Canon Rex Davis
  Rev. John Gunstone
* Rt Rev. Richard Hare
    Bishop of Pontefract
  Rev. Michael Harper
* Miss Janet Henderson
* Rev. Michael Hodge

* Miss Christian Howard
* Sister Irene Benedict
  Rev. David McInnes
* Rev. Brian Masters
* Mrs Jean Mayland
  Mrs Rachel Moss
* Rev. Reg Priestnall
* Rev. Michael Rees
  Rev. John Richards
  Rev. Tom Smail
* Canon Ivor Smith-Cameron
* Miss Jinny Wade

(* Synod member)

Ecumenical Guests:
Rev. Dr Gunnars Ansons (Lutheran)
Rev. Dr David Russell (Baptist)
Rev. Emmanuel Sullivan (Roman Catholic)
Dr Andrew Walker (Russian Orthodox)

General Synod Staff:
Mr Derek Pattinson
Mr Brian Hanson
Rev. David Gregg

In a context of worship and informal fellowship the following papers were presented, formally responded to, and discussed:

I 'A factual presentation of the history of the present movement within the Church of England and a survey of its present extent.' by the Rev. John Richards — responded to by Miss Christian Howard.

II 'An impressionistic view of the influence of Charismatic Renewal in the life of the Church of England.' by the Rev. (now Canon) John Gunstone — responded to by Canon Ivor Smith-Cameron.

III 'Questions raised for the historic Churches by the advent of the Charismatic Movement.' by the Rev. Dr David Russell — responded to by Canon Rex Davis.

IV 'Psychological aspects of the Charismatic Renewal Movement.' by Dr Bill Allchin — responded to by the Rev. Tom Smail.

The consultation made three recommendations, *asking* that a report of the consultation be prepared; *suggesting* the setting up of a small working group to prepare 'a popular report to promote discussion in the Church at large', based on the report of the Ely Consultation; and *identifying,* in the light of the ecumenical significance of the movement and its implications for mission and evangelism, the Board for Mission and Unity as the most appropriate agency of the Synod to take the matter further, perhaps in the wider context of spirituality as a whole. These recommendations were subsequently accepted by the Policy Sub-Committee of the Standing Committee, and a small working group was set up. Its composition and task is described in the Foreword of this, its eventual report.

More on 'Baptism in the Spirit'

We offer the following material, and that in the two succeeding appendices on 'the Gift of Tongues' and on 'Prophecy', as a basis for further study of these subjects (which could be pursued either individually or in a group).

THE NEW TESTAMENT EVIDENCE
We note the following passages, often cited by members of the Charismatic Movement, in which baptism is specifically linked with the Holy Spirit: (i.e. This is a broader selection than just the passages recording the phrase 'Baptism in/with the (Holy) Spirit', but, on the other hand, it is *not* a comprehensive treatment of the New Testament teaching on the Holy Spirit.)

(a) John's baptism with water contrasted with that of Jesus with the Holy Spirit.
    (i) By John. Matt. 3.1-12 Mk. 1.4-8 Lu. 3.7-17
                Jo. 1.19-34 (and cf. 3.22-30 and 4.1,2).
    (ii) By Jesus. Acts 1.1-11
    (iii) By Peter. Acts 11.16
    (iv) By Paul (?) — see (h) below.

(b) The Holy Spirit descending on Jesus at his baptism
    Matt. 3.13-17 Mk. 1.9-11 Lu. 3.21, 22.

(c) The 'Great Commission'. Matt. 28.19.

(d) Peter's exhortation on the Day of Pentecost. Acts 2.37-42.

(e) The ministry of Philip, Peter and John in Samaria. Acts 8.9-25.

(f) The baptism of Paul. Acts 9.17-19.

(g) The baptism of Cornelius and his household. Acts 10.23-48.

(h) Paul baptizing the dozen men at Ephesus. Acts 19.1-7. (With the preceding account of Apollos's defective understanding, this may also constitute an example of (a) above.)

(i) As the basis of Paul's plea for unity in the Spirit?
    I Cor. 12.1-31 (esp. v.13) and cf. Eph. 4.1-16 (esp. vv. 3-5).

(j) Brought together in a catalogue of the marks of the Christian?
    Heb. 6.1-6.

(Additional to our treatment of this subject on pp. 30, 31)

(a) We note that there are no specific Old Testament antecedents for the linking of baptism with the Holy Spirit. Indeed 'baptism' only occurs in a relevant context at all in the story of Naaman (2 Ki. 5.14), and that is without any reference to the Spirit. Paul admittedly sees some analogy with the crossing of the Red Sea (I Cor. 10.1-16), but generally it may be said that the whole concept is part of the *newness* of the New Testament.

(b) We find the matter alluded to in all four Gospels at some length, and a prominent feature of Acts. We must therefore conclude that it is an important and central theme, and *not* just an interesting but secondary matter.

(c) On the strictest analysis the only true use of the term 'baptism in the Spirit' is that which is found in the predictions of the Baptist and in the fulfilment (usually with speaking in tongues) in Acts 2 (Jerusalem), Acts 8 (Samaria), and Acts 10 and 19 (Gentiles). It is not a term used directly in relation to other converts or found anywhere in the Pauline Corpus. However, we feel it would be misleading to confine consideration of the subject solely to verbal links between baptism and the Spirit. Many other passages (e.g. Jesus breathing on the disciples — Jo. 20.22, or the account of what befell them on the Day of Pentecost — Acts 2.1-13, or the use of the phrase '. . . .filled with the Holy Spirit' in various places) are clearly relevant to the discussion of this phenomenon.

(d) It is not possible to systematize too precisely the references cited. We find examples of the Spirit falling upon some without any reference to baptism. We find some who are baptized and no reference made to the Spirit. Sometimes the Spirit comes with the laying on of hands. Etc. etc.

We conclude, therefore, that (in the phrase recorded of Jesus) 'the Spirit blows where it wills . . .' (Jo. 3.8). But we note a strongly emphasized *connection* in the New Testament between water baptism and the coming of the Spirit, and also an incontrovertible use of the *imagery* of baptism (i.e. being 'dipped' or 'immersed in') to describe the early Christians' *experience* of the Spirit. Further, we see clear evidence, both by inference (Acts 8.14-24) and expressly (Lu. 11.13), that it is appropriate for Christians specifically to seek for, and to ask God for, the gift of the Holy Spirit. Nevertheless, we question whether these passages really justify the significance placed upon them by some exponents of Charismatic renewal.

A MAJOR POINT OF DEBATE

Many find under this phrase 'Baptism in/with the (Holy) Spirit' the chief point of theological debate. Catholic theologians will want to ask if what is really being spoken of is Christian Initiation. We note that most Anglican charismatics are now very cautious about any concept of a two-stage

57

initiation connected with their experience. The search for understanding is no doubt complicated for us by the two schools currently prominent in Anglican thinking on initiation namely (a) that Baptism and Confirmation and First Communion form a (sometimes drawn out) process of initiation, and (b) that Baptism alone constitutes the complete rite of initiation. Neither school however would wish to divorce the coming of the Holy Spirit from Baptism, since even those who hold (a) do not have a 'two-stage' view with the Holy Spirit only coming at the second.

We feel that recognition of the sacramental principle is essential. If it is true that 'All which God may give is vouchsafed in the one baptism', then it might be said that, in the 'Charismatic' experience, some have dramatically entered into a greater *fulness* of what their baptism signified. (This would inevitably provoke the question whether others are possibly 'missing out' on something.) We are quite clear, however, that neither the desire for the experience, nor the experience itself can in any way justify a second (or re-) baptism.

QUESTIONS FOR DISCUSSION

(a) Is the experience of the Holy Spirit that 'Charismatics' describe to be equated with the experience of the first Christians?

(b) What are we to make of the phrase in some of the passages cited 'Baptized in/with the Holy Spirit'?

(c) What is the relationship between water baptism and 'Spirit baptism'?

(d) Should *all* Christians be seeking the 'gift of the Holy Spirit', and, if so, how?

(e) How does all this relate to the Church of England's understanding and practice of Baptism and Confirmation?

FOR FURTHER READING

J. G. D. Dunn: *Baptism in the Holy Spirit.* SCM (London) 1970.
Michael Green: *I Believe in the Holy Spirit.* Hodder (London) 1975.
J. R. W. Stott: *Baptism and Fulness.* IVP (London) 1976.

More on 'the Gift of Tongues'

(For explanation, see the first paragraph of Appendix 3.)

THE NEW TESTAMENT EVIDENCE

The use of the word *glōssa* for unintelligible sounds uttered under the influence of the Holy Spirit is confined to the following New Testament passages:

(a) of the Disciples on the day of Pentecost. Acts 2.1-21

(b) of Cornelius and his household. Acts 10.44-48

(c) of the dozen men at Ephesus. Acts 19.1-6.

(d) Specific teaching, in the context of Paul's instructions about the use of spiritual gifts (I Cor. 12. 13, 14 *passim*).

In addition, it is also found

(e) Linked with baptism, in Mark 16.16, 17 — in a passage judged by most to be a later addition to Mark's gospel, possibly simply summarising the features of 'Acts'.

SOME OBSERVATIONS ON THESE PASSAGES

(Additional to the treatment of this subject on pp. 31, 32)

(a) Again, we find no specific Old Testament antecendents for this phenomenon, and neither do we find it mentioned in the gospels (unless we count Mk. 16.17). It appears therefore to be something particularly connected with the 'coming' of the Holy Spirit in the 'Pentecost' mode. We note however, some unique features of the phenomenon recorded in Acts 2, which some have seen as a reversal of the Tower of Babel. At the very least, there are implications in this passage of a direct apprehending, in recognizable language, of the intellectual content of the tongue-speaking which is missing from the other New Testament accounts. This direct evangelistic aspect in a cosmopolitan crowd poses problems for those who would wish to see the actual 'Pentecost' manifestation of speaking in tongues as normative. We note also a marked contrast between *all* the references in Acts, which show 'tongues' to be a *corporate* experience, and those in I Corinthians, which are much more *individualistic*.

(b) Since 'speaking in tongues' is directly attributed to the activity of the Holy Spirit in several places in the passages cited, and is also specifically stated to be *evidence* that the Holy Spirit *has come* (e.g. Acts 10.46 — and is this what lies behind Acts 8.17, 18?) we would find it difficult to gainsay that 'speaking in tongues' *is* an authentic and proper Christian experience/activity. However, in view of the relative paucity of the references to it, and in the spirit of the old adage that 'All dogs are animals, but *not* all animals are dogs!' we would find it unnecessary to assert that *all* Christians need to exhibit *this* gift to authenticate their discipleship, anymore than they *need* to be prophets, healers, miracle-workers, etc. (or *even* Church Administrators! — cf. Ro. 12.8).

(c) We are encouraged in this judgement by Paul's treatment of the subject in I Corinthians 12-14. It would appear that this gift was highly over-rated and abused in the Church in Corinth, possibly because it is a marked manifestation of the initial effervescence of the Spirit, whose novelty-value had not worn off in this immature church. We would feel that, if what is manifested today *is* to be equated with the New Testament phenomenon, and if it is regulated in public worship in the way that Paul advises, it can play a part in the building up of the body of Christ, and that its exercise in private can assist the individual in his or her pilgrimage — providing always that it is subject to the law of love (I Cor. 13). We *do* confirm that, like vocal, articulate prayer, it can have its place, given the inescapable pluriformity of Christian experience, in both public and private worship. But we firmly resist any suggestion that it ought to be an invariable.

(d) We find helpful the following assertion by an exponent of glossolalia, quoted in *The Charismatic Movement,* edited by Michael Hamilton (Eerdmans: Grand Rapids 1975. p.32):

> 'Christian speaking in tongues is done as objectively as any other person speaking, while the person is in full possession and control of his wits and volition, and in no strange state of mind whatever.'

(e) Finally, we note the close link made between 'Speaking in Tongues' and 'Prophecy' (e.g. Acts 2.15-21, Acts 19.1-6 and I Cor. 14) and even that 'interpreted' tongues may be *equated* with prophecy (I Cor. 14.5). This may help us to adjudge better what is *meant* by 'prophecy' — the subject of Appendix 5.

QUESTIONS FOR DISCUSSION

(a) Is the experience of 'speaking in tongues' which Charismatics claim, to be equated with the experience attested to in these passages cited?

(b) What should be the attitude towards 'speaking in tongues' of a modern Christian who has not (yet?) experienced it?

(c) Is this a 'gift' that is given permanently, or is it only an initiation experience which gradually dies away?

FOR FURTHER READING

Don Basham: *The Miracle of Tongues.* Revel (Old Tappan) 1973.

J.G.D. Dunn: *Jesus and the Spirit.* SCM (London) 1975.

A. C. Thiselton: art. The 'interpretation' of tongues? in *Journal of Theological Studies* n.s. 30. 1979.

More on 'Prophecy'

(For explanation, see first paragraph of Appendix 3.)

THE NEW TESTAMENT EVIDENCE

Unlike the subjects of the other two appendices (3 and 4) where the New Testament evidence is fairly limited, references to prophecy and to prophets abound. The following references are therefore selective. We adduce some main passages, and then list some more isolated points:

(a) Prophecy directly related to the influence of the Holy Spirit. Acts. 2.16-21, 2 Pet. 1.17-21, (and cf. Lu. 1.67, Acts 11.28, I Cor. 12.10).

(b) One of the *charismata*. I Cor. 12-14 *passim* (and cf. Acts 19.6, Ro. 12.6, I Thess. 5.20?)

(c) False prophets. Mt. 7.15-23, 2 Pet. 2.1-22.

(d) The prophecy of the two witnesses. Rev. 11.1-13.

(e) Generalised references. Mt. 10.41, 13.57, Lu. 13.33 Eph. 2.20 (where the prophets referred to are almost certainly contemporaries).

(f) A means of discerning the will of God. I Tim. 1.18, 4.14.

(g) Specific New Testament prophets (male and female) identified. Acts. 11.27, 15.32, 21.9 (and Titus 1.12?)

(h) As a general self-description of the Book of Revelation. Rev. 1.3 (10.11?) and 22.7, 10, 18, 19.

(i) New Testament fulfilment of Old Testament prophecy. Mt. 13.14, 15.7, I Pet. 1.10.

(j) The Jewish leaders' challenge to Jesus. Mt. 26.68 (and //s.)

(k) The High Priest's prophecy. Jo. 11.47-53.

(l) Implication of normality for both men and women? I Cor. 11.4, 5.

SOME OBSERVATIONS ON THESE PASSAGES

(Additional to the treatment of this subject on p. 33)

(a) Unlike our previous two subjects (Appendices 3 and 4) Old Testament antecedents to the theme of 'prophecy' abound. Abraham is spoken of as the first prophet (Gen. 20.7), though it is Moses who is normative (Deut. 18.15-19 and 34.10). From his time onwards prophets and prophecy become a major feature. We note particularly the Hebrew tradition which designates the books of Joshua, Judges, Samuel and Kings as the 'former prophets' — paying special attention to Samuel, Elijah and Elisha — as well as grouping the written prophecies of Isaiah, Jeremiah etc, as the 'latter prophets'. It is the LORD who *makes* prophets, so that phrases like 'The

Word of the LORD came to me' or 'The Spirit of the LORD was upon me' become indicative, (e.g. I Sam. 10.1-13) and prophecy is often given in first person speech 'I, the LORD, say unto you' etc. The function of prophecy is to interpret history and current events, and to voice ethical and social judgements. Various modes of communication are found, including visions, dreams and acted parables, as well as symbolic and verbal utterances.

(b) Some see prophecy as the strongest point of continuity between Old Testament and New Testament. As well as Jesus' own attitude to the prophets, he himself is seen as the greatest of them. The main emphasis at Pentecost is on this theme (from Joel); John the Baptist is a specific link (Mt. 11.13); Prophetic utterances are attributed to Zechariah, Anna, Simeon and Mary at the time of Jesus' birth etc. etc. There seems no evidence to suggest *any* sort of discontinuity at all, therefore, between the Old Testament concept of 'prophecy' and that found in the New Testament. In the listing of prophecy amongst the gifts of the Spirit; in the assertion that every Christian is potentially a prophet (I Cor. 14.31) (and we note that this *includes* women — cf. I Cor. 5.31, 11.5, 12.11 etc. and see Acts 21.9); and in the actual identifying of New Testament prophets as such, the concept is all of a piece with that of the Old Testament.

(c) We note the specific link made between 'Baptism in the Spirit' and 'Speaking in tongues' with 'Prophecy'. The major impression is that 'prophecy' has the pre-eminence, perhaps amongst all the gifts of the Spirit. (Although we note the priority given to Apostles in I Cor. 12 and Eph. 2.20, pointing perhaps to a basic 'test' of authentic prophecy i.e. whether it accords with the apostolic teaching.) Prophecy is thus, for some, *the* crucial practical aspect of the Charismatic movement, and therefore the most controversial. We feel we cannot rightly ask *'Is* there such a thing?' Clearly there is. But we must ask 'What is it?' 'How do we recognise it?' 'How do we test it?'

(d) 'Guidance' under the Holy Spirit can take many forms. 'Prophecy' may occur without being identified as such (or being dignified as 'Thus says the LORD . . .'), although the same process of waiting on the Holy Spirit in prayer, and then finding that someone 'sees the way through', may be involved. We also believe that division of opinion, or lack of agreement in, say, a PCC on what is the right way ahead, may be just as much due to inadequate personal relationships as to a failure on the part of some to discern the voice of God in an alleged 'prophecy'. And we see the danger of domination by strong-minded personalities, or a propensity to look for 'short-cut' answers in some attitudes to this gift. We feel therefore that the application of certain tests for *true* prophecy is of crucial importance.

(e) It is with this question of testing that we would wish to conclude. We detect at least four tests that can and should be applied.

(i) Does the 'prophecy' conform to the teaching of the Scriptures?

(ii) Does it bring forth appropriate 'fruits', for instance in the fostering of love and in the building up of the fellowship?

(iii) Does it commend itself to the consensus of the duly appointed leaders/elders of the congregation where it is given?

(iv) Does it encourage the confession that 'Jesus is LORD'?

QUESTIONS FOR DISCUSSION

(a) What *is* 'prophecy'? How is it distinguished from preaching, teaching etc?

(b) Do you agree with the 'tests' suggested in (d) above? Are there any others to enable 'true' prophecy to be distinguished from 'false'. (How can you tell 'false' prophets?)

(c) Is the gift of prophecy a permanent gift for some, or is it 'ad hoc'?

FOR FURTHER READING

David Atkinson: *Prophecy*. Grove (Nottingham) 1977
Arnold Bittlinger: *Gifts and Ministries*. 1974
Michael Harper: *Prophecy*. Fountain Trust 1964.

The House Church Movement

Our report is focused on the Charismatic Movement *in the Church of England,* but we feel that a little more needs to be said about the House Church Movement. We note particularly the inevitable antithesis it presents to those who, whilst remaining loyal to the Church of England, have put emphasis on the importance of house *groups* in the working out of their Charismatic experience.

The following description of the movement is from a feature entitled *Who's Who in the House Church Movement,* compiled by the editor of *Crusade* magazine, Derek Williams, to accompany his article mentioned below, and is here reproduced by his kind permission:

The 'house church movement' is a loose umbrella title covering a variety of independent, charismatic groups: independent in the sense of being un-denominational, charismatic in the sense of exercising the spiritual gifts of tongues, prophecy and healing. Not all of them meet in houses.

George Tarleton's assertion that 'the house church movement is dead' is accepted by many within its ranks; in other words, the formative period is over and new developments are taking place. 'House churches' are increasingly joining together for worship in larger gatherings while some denominational churches are splitting up into smaller fellowship groups and meeting less regularly for corporate worship.

There are five discernible strands within the movement.

Long established independent groups. Some isolated house churches have existed for 15 years or more, but are unrelated to each other or the more recognisable groups. Their emphasis is on independence.

The 'Fullness group'. So called because of the title of its magazine, this is a loose federation of church leaders based on longstanding personal friendship and includes Gerald Coates, John Noble, Nick Butterworth, Graham Perrins and George Tarleton. They are the least organised of the house church groups, anxious to maintain flexibility and spontaneity. Their particular emphasis is on the prophetic ministry. Gerald Coates is the most public figure among them and his Kingdom Life meetings each year, in his home town of Cobham, attract around 2000 people from churches all over Surrey and neighbouring counties. He was also involved in the recent 'Bind us Together' musical tour.

The Harvestime (Bradford) Group. Based in Bradford, but with fellowships as far away as Brighton, this is a more closely organised group which does not always see eye to eye with the Fullness leaders. They have tended to buy up redundant churches, and have a stronger emphasis on discipline and submission to leaders. They hold commitment classes for new members, and are closest of all the groups to being a denomination. Ideas are disseminated through *Restoration* magazine, and leaders include Bryn Jones (often now in the USA), and well-known writer Arthur Wallis, with Dave Mansell in London and Terry

Virgo in Brighton. It is also the most flourishing of the groups, with its annual Dales Bible Week attracting 10,000 people to the Yorkshire Show Ground at Harrogate, and the Downs Bible Week in the south now attracting about 3000.

The Chard group. In the past this has been probably the most sectarian of the groups, and it has a strong disciplinary element. Its special emphases are on the overt charismatic ministries of deliverance and healing. Based on a small community at Chard in Somerset, it is led by Sid Purse, Vic Dunning and Ian Andrews.

Pastor North's groups. Nicknamed 'the North Circular' by others, it remains exclusive and rarely joins in fellowship with them. George ('Wally') North is its pastor, and confusion is sometimes created by his use of 'new birth' for what most others would call spiritual fullness. He takes the Wesley and Finney view on holiness and perfectionism.

(A fuller critique of the House Church Movement may be found in:
Derek Williams art. 'Denominations — the End of the Road?' in *Crusade,* January 1981.
Walter Hollenweger art. 'The House Church Movement in Great Britain' in *Expository Times,* November 1980.)